The Power of Speaking God's Word

Reformation & Revival Ministries

Reformation & Revival Ministries, in a partnership with Christian Focus Publications, began an imprint line of books in the year 2000 for the purpose of providing resources for the reformation of the Christian church through the life and work of Christian leaders. Our goal is to publish and distribute new works of pastoral and theological substance aimed at reforming the leadership, life and vision of the church around the world.

Reformation & Revival Ministries was incorporated in 1991, through the labors of John H. Armstrong, who had been a pastor for the previous twenty-one years, for the purpose of serving the church as an educational and evangelistic resource. The desire from the beginning has been to encourage doctrinal and ethical reformation joined with informed prayer for spiritual awakening. The foundational convictions of the ministry can be summarized in the great truths of the sixteenth century Protestant Reformation and the evangelical revivals of the eighteenth and nineteenth centuries.

To accomplish this vision the ministry publishes a quarterly journal (since 1992), *Reformation & Revival Journal*, designed for pastors and serious readers of theology and church renewal. A more popular magazine, *Viewpoint*, is published six times per year. The ministry also has an extensive array of books and tapes.

Dr. Armstrong speaks in conferences, local churches and various ministerial groups across the United States and abroad. The ministry has a no debt policy and is financed only by the gifts of interested people. The policy from the beginning has been to never ask for funds through solicitation, believing that God provides as he will, where he will, and when he will. An office and support staff operate the ministry in suburban Chicago.

Further information on the ministry and the above resources can be found in the following ways:

Reformation & Revival Ministries
P. O. Box 88216
Carol Stream, Illinois 60188
(630) 980-1810
(630) 980-1820, Fax

E-mail: RRMinistry@aol.com   Web: www.randr.org

The Power of Speaking God's Word

Wilbur Ellsworth

Christian Focus
Reformation and Revival Ministries

for Jean

'She speaks with wisdom
and faithful instruction is on her tongue'
Proverbs 31:26

ISBN 1 85792 604 8

Published in 2000 by
Christian Focus Publications, GeaniesHouse,
Fearn, Ross-shire, IV20 1TW, Great Britain

For a free catalogue of all our titles, please write to
Christian Focus Publications,
Geanies House, Fearn,
Ross-shire, IV20 1TW, Great Britain

For details of our titles visit us on our web site
http://www.christianfocus.com

Cover design by Owen Daily

Contents

Acknowledgments

It is the fondest hope of any writer that his work will be helpful to others. The reason I have such a hope is that so many people graciously helped me in the creation of this work. I am grateful to the people of the First Baptist Church in Wheaton, Illinois, for their support in resources, prayer, and allowing me the time for this project. I appreciate the guidance of Dr. David Larsen, who gave direction for the shape of this project and provided rich resources from his vast knowledge of the subject. I am thankful to my friend, Dr. John Armstrong, who believed in the value of this work and introduced it to Malcolm Maclean and Christian Focus Publications to be among the first of a series of books to be released under the Reformation and Revival imprint. Joanne Mcclelland deserves my unending thanks for hours and effort beyond my knowing for preparing the manuscript. Above all, I express my gratitude to my wife Jean who has made more contributions than I can tell. Without her this book would not exist.

Introduction

God's written word begins by describing the power of God's spoken word in the six days of creation. Six times we read, 'And God said...', and all creation came into being when God spoke. The prophets of Israel penetrated the darkened consciences of their people by proclaiming, 'This is what the Lord says.' Jesus Christ was committed to the power of his speech: 'The words I have spoken unto you are spirit and they are life.' Paul gave Timothy the mission for extending the Christian message to the next generation in his charge, 'Preach the word.' In the last direct word from God in the Bible it is written that the Lord Jesus says, 'Yes, I am coming soon.'

My purpose in writing this book has been to explore what the power of speaking God's word means for the preacher. Some have called this issue 'the orality of preaching', but outside North America I am told that orality is understood as being confined only to dental care! So before anyone consigns this book to dental libraries it will be important to define orality as communication that is spoken as distinguished from communication that is written. To put it another way, orality concerns words that are heard as distinguished from words that are seen.

Whatever else the preacher thinks about his work, the unique qualities of the spoken word and the demands and disciplines placed upon the oral communicator deserve his attention. Over the centuries of preaching, people have recognized that words on paper, even when they are words of sacred Scripture, are different from words on the lips of a living person. One old English preacher said it is not possible to carry fire in paper but that paper will do very well to light the fire. I must emphasize that at no point in describing the differences between the spoken and written word am I undermining a high view of Scripture. The trustworthiness and the authority of the Bible as given

7

by God to his people is assumed throughout. In fact, it is the Bible itself that describes speaking God's word in preaching as a Spirit-given act that drives and penetrates the written word into the inner beings of those who hear.

I encourage you to persevere in moving through the second chapter on the characteristics of orality. While the discussion of orality as being dialogical, communal, formulaic, descriptive, situational and acoustic may at first seem overly abstract, it is only as we begin to grasp the practical importance of these qualities that we begin to understand the practical decisions we must make in order to be effective speakers of God's word.

It is my hope that this work on the oral nature of preaching will be seen as far more than a communication technique or an engaging way to impress a congregation by the ability to speak without use of notes. There is far more involved than that. Preaching the word of God is God's way of communicating the truth that resides in his own life and bringing that truth to the inner lives of people made in his image through the humble vessels of his preachers. From beginning to end God's word is personal, alive and relational. The power of speaking God's word is found in maintaining that vision throughout the preaching work. It is my prayer that God will be pleased to use this book in the service of the speaking of his word in power.

CHAPTER 1

TALK IS NOT CHEAP!

A preacher talks. That apparent truism possesses formative power in understanding what really is involved in preaching. This book will explore the significance of preaching as an essentially oral act. The preacher's speech is the focal point of communicating what the preacher desires to convey. The complicating fact is that the preacher's talking is to be rooted in the written Scripture. The difference between written communication (literacy) and spoken communication (orality) calls for exploration in order to arrive at an understanding as to how each form of communication is to direct the preacher in the preaching act.

The orality of preaching is an issue that only gradually began to impress me as an important component in effective preaching. After nearly three decades of preaching, I was still wrestling with some unidentified quality that seemed to come and go unnoticed while directly influencing the impact of my sermons. Sermons that had been prepared carefully sometimes seemed to have a remoteness that would surface in congregational feedback. Other times, when careful preparation was impossible due to unexpected events, and the urgency and passion of the moment had to carry the day, congregational response was unusually positive.

A letter from a knowledgeable professional person in the congregation drove me to think again about my preaching. She wrote that shortly after leaving church she often could not remember some 80% of my sermons. However, she also observed that the remaining 20% often deeply impacted her life in ways that changed her walk with God. I found myself asking if there were any possible way to understand what the difference was. During the week before Easter in 1996, I contemplated this 'formidably forgettable' quality of my preaching as I prepared for one of the greatest preaching events of the year. I knew that, as always, a great many people would be in the morning services for a rare opportunity to hear the message of hope in Christ. I didn't want that event to be forgettable. I thought of the people who would be coming who were not usually in church and who needed to hear the gospel. I thought of the magnificent music that characterizes our Easter worship and I didn't want the ministry of God's Word to be overshadowed. Without any strong sense of purpose, I pulled down from the shelf an old book by Clarence Macartney, *Preaching Without Notes.*

While I had read the book many years earlier, I had not considered its earnest message very seriously. Looking back, I now realize that I had always had a rather dismissive view of a sermon that would be so loosely conceived that notes would not be necessary. Without consciously thinking it through, I had dismissed preaching without a written manuscript as being almost certain to be shallow, full of over-worn clichés and repetitious. Surely 'deep' teaching of God's Word required more support in the pulpit than my poor memory could provide. In fact, I had always been rather sceptical about the value of memory. Why labor over something to commit it to memory when it was always accessible in a book to be referred to again and again? I knew the kind of careful phrasing and intricate thought I valued could never be sustained by merely hoping to remember it. The thought of Sunday morning preaching of this sort 'felt' to me as though I was failing to offer my best to God.

And yet I knew I needed to do something different, and preaching in a direct manner to the congregation without being dependent on written support seemed to offer a significant way to explore what both I and at least some of my more vocal people in the congregation were seeking. So, knowing little about what I was doing, I tried to structure a message that was clear in its organization, descriptive in its illustrations, and capable of being remembered by a few 'memory signposts' that I could confine to a 'post-it' note in my Bible. The response was encouraging. I remember one extended family who had to be seated on the front row because of the crowd in the second service. Three generations were sitting there and the family had just lost a son in an accident only a few weeks earlier. The older parents were not evangelical nor particularly positive toward even being in church. They all listened carefully and I felt they never wandered in their attention. I became aware even while preaching that this kind of response would not have happened with my more precise manuscript-based sermons.

There have been no manuscripts since. 'Post-it' notes on the page of the biblical text have become the only memory help and, more recently, I have gradually moved out to stand in front of the pulpit for the entire sermon holding my Bible with only a post-it note inside. I read the text but rely on memory for other brief biblical citations. One of our pastors who has listened and thought through these questions with me for many years has said he would never have guessed so much effect could have come from a single change. Moving away from the pulpit in incremental stages until I now stand on a lower platform in front of it has probably been effective for two reasons: it removes the physical barrier between the preacher and the congregation and in our elongated sanctuary has removed a bit of spatial distance to the congregation. For me, the change really was not simple and the underlying factors in this change are still becoming clear as the process continues.

One of the factors which makes an oral approach to preaching important for me is that I have had a strong literary bent since my youth. Reading and books have been a strong source of pleasure from the time I learned to read. I tend to approach any issue by looking for the book which would best address that subject. Because I love the beauty of words and the snap of a well-turned phrase, the craft of being precise with words holds great fascination for me. I also find that my intuitive approach to thought makes my ideas and words rather complex and often

more full than precise. Those tendencies have created an innate
sense of dependence on a written support for preaching. The
preacher I listened to in my youth was well-read and delivered
carefully crafted sermons. His language was elevated and his
expressions were complex. I suspect those influences have
pressed me to walk in the same paths.

All this means that moving to a more orally oriented manner
of preaching is not a small step for me. The movement from the
literate roots of the Scripture and biblical studies to the
unadorned exposure of strong orality continues to be a journey
with new horizons continuing to appear. In retrospect I now
realize the roots of my seminary training tended to create
problems and tensions in my preaching as the orientation of
those years of study was intensely literary. I believe it is accurate
to say that while much of the seminary training was invaluable,
the values of oral communication were not presented. It is
important to note that I am writing this after having preached
for nearly thirty years. I have written many sermon manuscripts
and have profited from the discipline of seeking precision and
clarity in that process. For a young preacher to dispense with
the disciplines of writing could result in semi-formed expression
and may diminish what orality that moves out from literacy
could produce.

In this project I will explore the distinctive characteristics of
orality and the tensions that arise between orality and literacy
unless there is clear and intentional linkage between the two. I
will relate the biblical evidences that Christian revelation is both
an oral and a literary phenomenon and that the preacher must
be aware of how each aspect of preaching needs to relate to
both. I will argue that significant statements of Scripture strongly
suggest that orality is an important component in God's intended
process of his Word coming to impact people. With a brief
survey of preaching history I will demonstrate that many of the
great preachers in the Christian church have been orally-oriented
in their preaching, even though their enduring legacy to us comes
down in written form. I will deal with the practical issue of how

a sermon can remain oral in its delivery through an understanding of memory. It will be shown that oral communication that relies on memory is a sermonic form that begins at the earliest stages of sermon preparation and that sermon structure is an essential component of oral delivery. Finally, I will draw together the study, observation and experiences that have brought me to a growing respect for orality in preaching and how orality requires a lifelong discipline to develop this approach to preaching.

CHAPTER 2

WHAT IS ORALITY?

Author Kenneth Atchity once was introduced at a party to a producer as 'my friend the writer'. 'Oh,' said the producer, 'say something in writing.'[1] That amusing incongruity reflects the difference between communication through writing and through speech. How could the writer have responded? Certainly it would have been ludicrous for him to have pulled out a paper and continued his conversation by writing. Perhaps he might have first written down what he wanted to communicate to his new acquaintance and then read it. The question raises the issue of the relationship between written and spoken communication. When a writer is asked why she wrote a certain piece she might reply, 'Because I had something I wanted to say.' In that case, 'saying something in writing' makes rather clear sense. It suggests a desire to 'cut through', to express in a focused and personal way a message or an experience of significant meaning and to do so through the medium of writing.

Reflecting on the nature of orality requires a growing awareness of the diversity of orality and literacy within the means of communication. Robert Ensign observes that 'earlier generations of scholars assumed a large degree of equivalence between oral tradition and the written texts which derive from it'.[2] In more recent years that equivalence has become increasingly questioned. Orality has characteristics which, while not making it antithetical to literacy, do create important distinctions. Of paramount concern to the Christian are the implications of oral and literary distinctions on a high view of Scripture. The antecedent oral dynamics to the biblical text provide important insight concerning the nature of Scripture and biblical interpretation but need not diminish the historic orthodox view of inspiration. Belief in the inspiration of Scripture places high confidence in the Holy Spirit's guiding and protecting work to ensure accuracy and reliability that leaves a trustworthy record of God's Word. It is the Spirit's work to bridge the gap from orality to text in a way that maintains both dynamism and reliability. The Catholic scholar Walter Ong represents the historic view of Scripture when he writes:

> To the text of the Bible which has resulted, the Church has always given an immediate, unmediated kind of authority. Whatever explanation and interpretation the text may at one time or another require, the life of the Bible is in the biblical text, not in the oral antecedents and much less in later interpretations, however indispensable these may be.[3]

Ong notes that 'in antiquity it was not common practice for any but disgracefully incompetent orators to speak from a text prepared verbatim in advance'.[4] Indeed, the very practice of studying speeches has until recently required that what was first delivered orally be reduced to a written form, since a spoken word disappears as soon as it is uttered. The academic concerns in understanding oral communication seem to have clouded the strong distinction between orality and literacy in the history of public speaking. From my own seminary experience and the common testimony of my pastoral colleagues, it is rather clear that homiletical training has primarily been rooted in the literary studies of biblical texts with relatively little (or in my own experience no) attention to the indisputable fact that when a preacher stands before the congregation the act is going to be oral. Unless an outline is projected or printed notes are given to the congregation, the only means the preacher has to convey the message is the spoken word.

It is significant that while sermons based on rather fully developed written outlines or even complete manuscripts have formed a major part of recent decades in America, the demand for this practice to be changed is becoming increasingly emphatic. From my own preaching experience it seems to me that at least some of the criticism and disillusionment toward preaching may come from the failure of the preacher to understand the process of moving from the written foundations of preaching – the written Scripture and the written forms of sermon preparation – to the oral framework that the act of preaching requires.

One of the concerns that many pastors and teachers (I being one of them) have had in recent years is that our culture has been moving inexorably downward in its interest and ability to think and to wrestle with the larger thoughts and concerns that lie at the heart of any civilization. It is not inappropriate to fear the threat of 'dumbing down'. Articulate thinkers such as Neil Postman speak eloquently about 'amusing ourselves to death'.[5] While the present purpose is not to engage with Postman's alarm over the present media and image dominating communication revolution, it is important to note that the heart of his concern is the loss of regard for the word as the basis of communicating thought. While Postman makes a strong plea for the importance of retaining the values and contributions of the printed page, he is not seeking to diminish the value of oral communication.

The intention to retain the quality of oral communication is not to be confused with a reduction of intellectual intensity or the epistemological importance of the word. In parts of Christian academic circles there sometimes seems to be a low view of orality that sees the speaking context reducing the preacher's ability to communicate the biblical teaching our post-Christian generation desperately needs. While there is significant renewal of interest in oral preaching, a large portion of the ministerial training establishment has been rather dismissive of orality in preaching.

It does not require much of a search to discover that experts in the modern communication process fully respect the importance of orality in today's society. In observing the impact of technology on modern culture, Marshall McLuhan notes:

Literate people have great difficulty in approaching nonvisual spaces since they tend to accept the activity of the eye in isolation from the other spaces. Further, they assume that the Euclidean space created by the visual sense in isolation from the other senses is space itself. Under electric conditions, therefore, Western man is in a great state of confusion as he encounters the multiple forms of space generated by new technological environments. Literate and visually-oriented scientists in many fields, from mathematics to anthropology, make only the most oblique contact with other materials because of their unconscious visual orientation.... The return of the bardic tradition in the age of the Beatles and Joan Baez has created new problems in the study of English literature. Much modern poetry today is written to be sung. The boundaries between the written and the oral are becoming very elusive.[6]

This wide-ranging paragraph serves to suggest the great wave of issues coming to present day consciousness due to the new possibilities of technology, but underneath these issues lie some of the most profound issues of orality (sound orientation) and literacy (visual orientation).

In an article entitled 'Acoustic Space', Edmund Carpenter and Marshall McLuhan suggest some of the tensions between literacy and orality:

In our society, however, to be real, a thing must be visible, and preferably constant. We trust the eye, not the ear. Not since Aristotle assured his readers that the sense of sight was 'above all others' the one to be trusted, have we accorded to sound a primary role. 'Seeing is believing.' 'Believe half of what you see and nothing of what you hear.' 'The eyes of the LORD preserve knowledge, and he overthroweth the words of the transgressor' (Prov. 22:12). Truth, we think, must be observed by the 'eye', then judged by the 'I'.[7]

These statements serve to prepare the way to explore some of the foundational characteristics of orality in contrast to literacy, an aural versus a visual form of communication.

Orality is Dialogical

The dialogic character of orality confronts us in the partygoer's humorous request to 'say something in writing'. When one person speaks to another there is a 'face to face' encounter where personal contact and a sensitivity to interaction is not only important for effective communication, it is essential to common courtesy. Orality stands apart from written communication in the way the communication begins. Paul O'Neil, a writer for *Life* magazine, articulated what has become known as O'Neil's law: 'Always grab the reader by the throat in the first paragraph, sink your thumbs into his windpipe in the second and hold him against the wall until the tag line'.[8] Needless to say, while such advice is cleverly articulated writing counsel; it is criminal speech behavior! The dialogic nature of orality requires sensitivity in the introductory moment.

> Older homiletic texts seemed to suppose that the very first sentence of a sermon was a crucial 'grabber' that by sheer rhetorical force could instantly command audience attention. Evidence is to the contrary. People do not easily attend the first few sentences of a public address. Just as when we swing a camera on a scene, focus may be fuzzy before gradually clarifying, so the first two or three sentences in a sermon are seldom clearly heard – they are fuzzy.... Actually, whenever we begin a casual conversation with another person on the street, even someone who knows us well, at the outset, there will be a process of adjusting to our syntax. Thus, at the beginning of an introduction, the first two or three sentences cannot bear much weight. A wise preacher will keep the initial sentences of a sermon short, uncomplicated, and without much adjectival elaboration.[9]

This discussion of introductions merely indicates the important distinction between orality and literacy in even beginning to communicate. The speaker needs to prepare introductions carefully, not only in selecting an interesting and attractive way to begin talking about the subject, but also in creating the necessary ethos in which appropriate communication can be established between the preacher and the congregation. The spirit of dialogue must inform the oral task of preaching from its outset. Buttrick's comments on the conversational dynamic of the introduction should not discourage the preacher from careful crafting of the opening sentences. The plea is not for vague wandering, but for a sensitivity to the entry point of dialogue. While a larger audience may require intensified energy and enlarged actions, the quality of conversation should always shape the delivery.

In the body of the oral communication the speaker must be continually aware of any possible indication of the listeners' response to what is being said. Do facial expressions give any hint that people are understanding the message or is there a significant level of confusion or perplexity? An appropriate pause, or even the occasional question, 'Am I making sense?' may elicit enough response for the speaker to know that either more needs to be said, particularly whether more illustrative or descriptive language related to life situations would help, or that it is appropriate to move on. A more sensitive issue is whether or not the speaker is gaining audience agreement or that doubt and disagreement are growing as the speech goes on. While the speaker's knowledge of the expected audience should carefully inform the preparation process – by anticipating the initial level of agreement and the obstacles most likely needing to be overcome in the speech – it is still essential that the speaker make every effort to be sensitive to the audience's developing level of agreement or disagreement with the speech. Equally important is the question of whether the listeners are maintaining active interest in the speaker's words. 'Boring' and 'irrelevant' are tombstones cluttering the landscape of much speaking and preaching response today. The speaker must continually ask, 'Am I giving my listeners good and compelling reason to stay involved?' Body language in an increasingly uninhibited society usually gives the speaker all the information the he needs (or can bear!).

The conclusion of the speech must remain dialogical if there is to be anything more than the hope that the talk is coming to an end. Keeping the audience in a dialogue to the end is particularly important for an oral presentation. A dialogic mentality will invite the listener to share a common vision of the possibilities that are on the horizon if this message gains their positive response. Points of decision, commitment and action need to be gathered up from the body of the speech and reviewed to encourage a clear response. The resources available and the rewards that will come need to be asserted in a way that gains the listener's 'yes'. Orality requires the passion and the freedom to keep this dialogic dynamism flowing throughout.

Orality is Communal

Walter Ong, who has pioneered much of the contemporary thought about orality, graphically describes the contrasting nature of orality and literacy in the execution of the task:

> (T)he person to whom the writer addresses himself normally is not present at all. Moreover, with certain special exceptions, ... he must not be present. I am writing a book which will be read by thousands, or, I modestly hope, by tens of thousands. So, please, get out of the room, I want to be alone. Writing normally calls for some kind of withdrawal.[10]

Apart from the obvious necessity of preparing for oral communication, the presence of the hearers with the speaker is foundational to the event. The very opposite is true of literacy. The byword of the reading room is 'Quiet'. In order for the communication of a writer to have its commonly intended result, the readers of the writer's words will find a quiet place without the distraction of other people and will isolate themselves from the world around them and enter into a private, isolated and inward interaction with the writer's text. It is significant that while a gathering of listeners around a speaker is called an audience, there is no comparable collective term for those who read.

> The orator has before him an audience which is a true audience, a collectivity. 'Audience' is a collective noun. There is no collective noun for readers.... 'Readers' is a plural. Readers do not form a collectivity, acting here and now on one another and on the speaker as members of an audience do. We can devise a singularized concept for them, it is true, such as 'readership'.... But 'readership' is not a collective noun. It is an abstraction in a way that 'audience' is not.[11]

Any speaker who has faced a small, scattered audience in a large room has experienced the power and impact that the presence and nature of an audience has upon oral communication. The communal nature of orality requires the speaker's sensitivity and the skill to adjust to the existential quality of the audience in ways not demanded of the writer. In fact, the contrasting skill of the writer must be the ability to see his reader in the abstractions of various situations even though the chosen subject of the writing may bring to the writer's imagination a focus and framework for an intended 'readership'. The woman at her kitchen table, the student in a library, the commuter on the train, the invalid in bed – all these people in their isolated relationship to the writer may well be the people receiving his or her words. When reading a text publicly the speaker must make imaginative decisions concerning how that text should be read. Oral reading of Scripture, or any other text, should be conceived as a genre in its own right that has a specific purpose and legitimacy in specific communication situations. However, the issue of reading an entire speech or sermon is a different matter.

Ong suggests that in contrast to the concrete nature of orality's audience, the receivers of written communication must participate in a double fiction.

> What do we mean by saying the audience is a fiction? Two things at least. First, that the writer must construct in his imagination, clearly or vaguely, an audience cast in some sort of role – entertainment seekers, reflective sharers of experience ... inhabitants of a lost and remembered world of prepubertal latency,

... and so on. Second, we mean that the audience must correspondingly fictionalize itself. A reader has to play the role in which the author has cast him, which seldom coincides with his role in the rest of actual life.... Readers over the ages had to learn how to play the game of being a member of an audience that 'really' does not exist. And they have to adjust when the rules change, even though no rules thus far have ever been published and even though the changes in the unpublished rules are themselves for the most part only implied.[12]

This contrast between communal and privatized reception serves to explain the high importance given to application and relevance when a speaker's words are based on a written text such as the Bible. While the canonization of the Scripture is the church's confession that all Scripture is given for all the people of God at all times, the fact remains that we have written texts addressed to specific people at specific times and in specific situations that no longer exist. In order for preachers to communicate to a present audience, they must bring their listeners through a process of seeing how their present situation and the situation addressed in the text have a common bond. The cry for relevance in preaching is due largely to the fact that oral receivers expect specific concern for their situation whereas the reader knows that it may well be his or her responsibility to be able to imagine that link individually.

Orality is Formulaic

The deeply literate character of modern society is clearly seen in the widespread aversion to the idea of cliché.

Under the encouragement of I. A. Richards in his *Practical Criticism* as well as of other New Critics, clichés have for many years now been hunted down mercilessly with a view to total extermination, although of late the hunt has somewhat cooled, possibly because it itself has turned into a cliché.[13]

Writing has liberated speech from the necessity of using recognizable and stable forms and phrases because writing enables the reader to retain more diverse and creative expressions in a form that can be recalled through a text. Before the advent of writing, if any communication was to be retained and passed on, it had to be framed in ways that could be remembered. Clear structures, set phrases or aphorisms, and poetically expressive phrases became the roots of enduring speech. Ong analyzes the transforming power of writing on communication when he observes that 'talk, after writing, had to sound literate – and "literate", we must remind ourselves, means "lettered", or post-oral'.[14]

> After writing, in other words, oral speech was never the same. In one way it was better off. For in speaking, the mind could now go through motions of the kind men had learned from using writing. Moreover, you could, and did, use writing to make notes to help your speech. But in another way oral speech was worse off. It was now regularly compared with writing. It was no longer itself, no longer self-contained. Men were aware that there were many things that writing could do verbally which oral performance could not do at all. Oral performance no longer dominated the verbal field.[15]

Later in this project I will explore some of the implications of memory and oral speech. But for the present it is sufficient to note the common fear or frustration that a speaker faces at the thought of giving an extended public speech without notes. It is the simple problem of being unable to remember what needs to be said. This inability to remember the content to be spoken goes to the heart of the oral/literate dichotomy. Written speech flows on in sentences that become paragraphs that become chapters. While the topic sentence at the head of a paragraph is a recognized element of written speech, it does not necessarily have to be searingly memorable to be acceptable. A written topic sentence simply needs to state the idea clearly. An oral topical sentence must do far more. It must state the idea clearly, tersely, descriptively and formulaically so that not only does the thought become memorable by being part of a larger pattern (such as parallel construction); it must also have an intrinsic memorable quality in its own right, such as sharply descriptive nouns and verbs that make the milestones of the speech's progression stand out clearly. These elements must be couched in a simple and direct expression that flows naturally in the stream of *ex tempore* language so that a sharply literate tone does not intrude into the oral flow. The only pegs of memory for either the speaker or the listener are the innate memorability of the words chosen. This requires the speaker to develop the art of formulaic speech in such a way that the memory is served without the literate sensibilities of our present culture being disturbed.

Walter Ong explains the importance of formulaic speech patterns in cultures where the written text does not exist:

> How could you ever call back to mind what you had so laboriously worked out? The only answer is: Think memorable thoughts.... (Y)ou have to do your thinking in mnemonic patterns, shaped for ready oral recurrence. Your thought must come into being in heavily rhythmic, balanced patterns, in repetitions or antitheses, in alliterations and assonances, in epithetic and other formulary expressions, in standard thematic settings (the assembly, the meal, the duel, the hero's 'helper', and so on), in proverbs which are constantly heard by everyone so that they come to mind readily and which themselves are patterned for retention and ready recall, or in other mnemonic form. Serious thought is intertwined with memory systems.[16]
>
> In an oral culture, to think through something in non-formulaic, non-patterned, non-mnemonic terms, even if it were possible, would be a waste of time, for such thought, once worked through, could never be recovered with any effectiveness, as it could be with the aid of writing.[17]

When I reflect on the occasions when I have sat through the reading of a scholarly paper, with its thick and involved thought without any particular concern for either the speaker's need to remember the content without the text nor the audience's ability to follow or retain the content, it is not difficult to value the importance that oral culture has for the listener.

When contemporary speakers attempt to speak without written supports before them, the common experience is that of memory overload. Literary forms of speech simply overwhelm the memory capacity of most people. Furthermore, when exact recall of a written text is conceived as the desired goal, much of the oral quality is lost because the dialogic nature of communication has given way to a monologic remembrance of a written event. Until the appropriateness of the formulaic art is restored to the oral aspirations of speakers, the thought of speaking without resorting to notes will be an often honored but rarely experienced ideal. It should be remembered, however, that there is a counterbalancing influence common in society today that makes the formulary far from dead. Ong points to the cult of folk culture, the western movie, the in-group type of joke and most supremely the slogan, catch phrase or compulsive jingle.

> The advertising cliché is not in fact much of a knowledge storage and retrieval device at all. It is a slogan, which is not at all the same thing. The formulary devices of a primary oral culture are conservative devices, ordered to the treasuring and use of hard-earned lore. Slogans, by contrast, are typically action-oriented, fitted to short-term goals. The slogan enters more directly into the spirit of the new orality.[18]

While's Ong's point is that the cliché and slogan have a very different use in orality than in a literate setting, the case can be made that formula is still present and can be used artfully. While contemporary culture does recognize some value in oral formulaic speech, the skilful joining of analytic thought, that is more in keeping with literacy, and the patterned and aphoristic style of orality retain the possibilities for art in oral construction.

The 'sound bite mentality', so decried in thoughtful circles today, points to the creative tension between the memorable and the analytical. The objection is not the intelligent and creative use of formulae, but rather the use of formulaic speech as a substitute for thought. Artistic use of formulae as a framework for conveying a thoughtful message with integrity is still the only real way of conveying memorable truth with orality.

Orality is Concrete and Descriptive
One of the great contributions of literacy is the ability to 'break up' thought into smaller pieces, to analyze it with far greater focus and detail than is possible with oral communication. While reading a written text a person may move ahead in the flow of thought, confident that should the reader become confused or distracted or forgetful of something past in the text, it is possible to go back over the previous text selectively.

> In oral discourse, the situation is different. There is nothing to backloop into outside the mind, for the oral utterance has vanished as soon as it is uttered. Hence, the mind must move ahead more slowly, keeping close to the focus of attention much of what it has already dealt with.[19]

This necessity to 'keep close to the focus of attention' requires that oral communication maintain careful ties to what can be quickly assimilated into the hearer's experience and thought. Ong states: 'Oral cultures tend to use concepts in situational, operational frames of reference that are minimally abstract in the sense that they remain close to the living human lifeworld.'[20]

Ong reports on the work of A. R. Luria, who did extensive fieldwork with illiterate peasants in remote areas of the Soviet Union. He summarizes Luria's findings with these observations:

> (1) Illiterate (oral) subjects identified geometrical figures by assigning them the names of objects, never abstractly as circles, squares, etc. A circle would be called a plate, sieve, bucket, watch,

or moon; a square would be called a mirror, door, house, apricot drying board.

(2) Subjects were presented with drawings of four objects, three belonging to one category and the fourth to another, and were asked to group together those that were similar or could be placed in one group or designated by one word. One series consisted of drawings of the objects hammer, saw, log, hatchet. Illiterate subjects consistently thought of the group not in categorical terms (three tools, the log not a tool) but in terms of practical situations – 'situational thinking'– without adverting at all to the classification 'tool' as applying to all but the log.

(3) (H)is illiterate subjects seemed not to operate with formal deductive procedures at all – which is not the same as to say that they could not think or that their thinking was not governed by logic, but only that they would not fit their thinking into pure logical forms, which they seemed to have found uninteresting. Why should they be interesting? Syllogisms relate to thought, but in practical matters no one operates in formally stated syllogisms. (He contrasts the syllogism to the real-life orientation of the riddle, where one draws on knowledge, often deeply subconscious, beyond the words themselves in the riddle.)

(4) In Luria's field work, requests for definitions of even the most concrete objects met with resistance. 'Try to explain to me what a tree is.' 'Why should I? Everyone knows what a tree is, they don't need me telling them.... Why define, when a real-life setting is infinitely more satisfactory than a definition?... There is no way to refute the world of primary orality. All you can do is walk away from it into literacy.'

(5) Luria's illiterates had difficulty in articulate self-analysis. Self-analysis requires a certain demolition of situational thinking. It calls for isolation of the self, around which the entire lived world swirls for each individual person, removal of the center of every situation from that situation enough to allow the center, the self, to be examined and described.[21]

These qualities of oral thought – concreteness, situational orientation, practicality, reliance on description rather than definition, self-awareness as part of the social network rather than isolation – have profound implications even in our highly literate culture when we begin to grapple with what people require of those who communicate to them orally. Abstractions and analytical thinking, which literacy has introduced, have made both technology and many of the academic disciplines possible, but such abstractions have also made much of contemporary oral communication seem less than intellectually valid to the more highly developed intellectual segment of society. Ong reflects on the passing of rhetorical concerns from academic textbooks by the sixteenth century.

> The three *Rs* – reading, 'riting, and 'rithmetic – representing an essentially non-rhetorical, bookish, commercial and domestic education, gradually took over from the traditional orally grounded, heroic, agonistic education that had generally prepared young men in the past for teaching and professional, ecclesiastical, or political public service.[22]

Ong develops the tendency of literacy to overpower orality:

> Writing ... is a particularly pre-emptive and imperialist activity that tends to assimilate other things to itself even without the aid of etymologies. Though words are grounded in oral speech, writing tyrannically locks them into a visual field forever.[23]

This sense of 'fixity' tends to give literacy an aura of much higher reliability than what attends orality. The written or printed word 'is here to stay', while the spoken word lasts only in the moment of vibrating air or in the hearer's memory. Modern culture also has come to highly prize the enormous worth of literacy to create more abstract and particularlized thought than is possible in orality and it is this ability that has created the technology of the modern scientific age.

> Oral cultures indeed produce powerful and beautiful verbal performances of high artistic and human worth, which are no longer even possible once writing has taken possession of the psyche.

Nevertheless, without writing, human consciousness cannot achieve its fuller potentials, cannot produce other beautiful and powerful creations. In this sense, orality needs to produce and is destined to produce writing. Literacy ... is absolutely necessary for the development not only of science but also of history, philosophy, explicative understanding of literature and of any art (including oral speech itself).[24]

This is particularly true in academia and characterizes a significant part of seminary culture. The majority of seminary curriculum is highly literate and abstract. The study of theology, church history, biblical languages and exegesis are all textually based fields. Without question, these are highly important and essential areas of study for pastoral preparation. But however highly we value the benefits that literacy has brought to our culture, the concrete and descriptive nature of oral communication is still an essential issue for the public speaker and preacher. In fact, our increasing technology seems to create an even greater need for human touch and the human voice speaking to the human heart.

The current call for narrative preaching, with the rising popularity of the storyteller, supports the premise of John Naisbitt's famous title: 'From Forced Technology to High Tech/ High Touch'.[25] Narrative may be seen as simply an extended form of description. The story of a person's life, events that serve to create awareness of a specific idea or value, are all ways of communicating to people in ways that are both memorable and impacting to both speaker and hearer. Naisbitt's observation is one that bears the weight of common human experience: no matter how technological we become and how dependent we are on highly sophisticated ways to communicate, there is something undeniably strong in the human spirit that still requires the personal touch of one person talking to another and either telling, hearing or sharing in a significant story.

For the preacher, even the most theologically demanding texts of the Bible ultimately gain their power from unpacking technical terms and translating them into the situations and stories of life that touch not only the mind but the imagination. For example, the concept of propitiation leads the preacher to ask if God truly does have anger toward sin and sinners. Did Jesus on the cross actually face the anger of God? Going back into biblical stories and showing the distinction between immoral anger and righteous anger is a descriptive way a congregation will hear this teaching with involvement and remembrance.

Even though the technology of literacy has deeply impacted the human mind, the essential nature both of the human mind and spirit still retains strong ties with the values of orality. Defending the validity of image-oriented orality, Clyde Fant writes:

> Image-oriented preaching more nearly corresponds to reality than our efforts to reduce reality to abstract absolutes. Definition is not superior to description in preaching, nor is the tightly argued, analytically ordered message superior to a more descriptive one. Austin Farrer says in *A Rebirth of Images*, 'There is a current and exceedingly stupid doctrine that symbol evokes emotion and exact prose states reality. Nothing could be further from the truth: exact prose abstracts from reality, symbol presents it.'[26]

Although definition is important in clear communication, the abstract categories of the literate culture often do not touch the human person as fully, deeply or enduringly as the personal qualities of orality. In fact, when the listener to a speech or sermon is compelled to take careful and copious notes to comprehend and retain what the speaker has said, the result, whether consciously intended or not, is to return communication from orality to literacy as quickly as possible. Abstraction may create a tension between literacy and orality that, if not kept in careful boundaries, creates a hybrid that fails to accomplish the ultimate effectiveness intrinsic to either orality or literacy.

A sensitivity that will prove to be more helpful to an effective speaker is the distinction between definition and description. While both have value in effective communication, at least the nuance should never be far from the speaker's thought. Our scientifically oriented culture has placed a high value on definition. It could be argued that the intellectual reductionism current in our age values only that which can be defined as real. We demand facts, statistics and precisely accurate definitions in our technological age, but when the speaker wishes to bring an audience to a point of view and to action, description, more than definition, will prove to be the more effective servant to that goal. 'Now faith is being sure of what we hope for, and certain of what we do not see', is commonly understood as a description of faith rather than a formal definition (Heb. 11:1). Indeed, it tends to disappoint as a definition, but creates an evocative foundation that requires imaginative development into more concrete description than the text itself provides.

Orality Is Situational
A further aspect of orality's concrete nature is that it happens within a specific situation that the speaker must not only take into account, but may also remark on so that the hearers are able to gain a sense of the order and setting required to enter into a communicational relationship. For instance, the situation of a Sunday morning sermon in a church where the congregation routinely gathers and where preacher and congregation are well known to each other requires very little reference to the situational context. The preacher may appropriately begin with the subject. However, if the preacher is a guest or is new to the congregation, orality requires the preacher to devote some part of the beginning of the sermon to establish rapport and acceptance in the minds of the hearers. If a significant event has occurred and is occupying the consciousness of the congregation, or if some attention-riveting occurrence takes place during the speech, orality will respond to and recognize that event, if for no other reason than to regain the audience's focused attention. This sense of occasion is foundational to oral effectiveness.

A speaker must sense and appropriately relate to the mood of the audience, as specifically as changing the opening words in order to reflect what has happened immediately preceding the beginning of the sermon. The sense of situation also concerns the motivation the speaker gives to the audience as to why *this subject* is significant *for us now*. It is significant that thoughtful and highly literate people decry the increasing demand of congregations to hear preaching that concerns where they are living now and not some remote and abstract doctrine that they see to be unrelated to their lives. The responsibility of the speaker is to take what may at first seem arcane and remote and create awareness that this issue is in fact very important to these listeners. The oral communicator can never be put off by the listeners' question, 'Why are we talking about this now?' Answering that question is not merely giving way to an immature demand for instant application. It is profoundly biblical, for no biblical theme was ever raised in Scripture without there being a pressing need among the people to whom it was addressed.

Situational sensitivity considers that the communication of the speaker is directed to the hearers in their present context and actively reflects awareness of, concern for, and relevance to that situation. A written text is commonly focused on a subject that the writer wishes to develop without relating to the situation of the reader or readers. This is a fundamental difference the oral communicator must never let get far from mind. While the reader may be willing to create an imaginary situation where the reading of a text may some day be important, the same grace is rarely given by a listener in an oral setting.

Orality Is Acoustic
I have placed the acoustic character of orality later in this order of description in order to allow the accumulative nature of orality's other characteristics to inform this part of the discussion. The exceedingly obvious fact that orality deals with sound rather

than sight, with the ear rather than the eye, should not be allowed to diminish the power of this issue. Brigance writes:

> There are sharp and important differences between the use of written word and the use of spoken words. These differences grow out of the fact that one style is intended for the eye and the other for the ear. The reader may absorb at leisure; the hearer must take it on the wing. The reader proceeds at his own pace; the hearer at the pace of the speaker. The reader may pause to think; to re-read; to consult, if necessary, a dictionary; the hearer must ever move onward without a pause, for if he stops to reflect on what has been said, the speaker leaves him behind, and the connection is broken. In short, the difference between written and spoken style is this: Written style must be ultimately intelligible to the reader. Spoken style must be *instantly intelligible* to the hearer.[27]

The necessity of instant intelligibility depends on several further specific qualities. Oral speech requires an artistic balance of repetition and restatement without any sacrifice to energy and movement.[28] Density of content is a major difference between appropriate oral and literary communication. In fact, the necessity of giving more mental space in orality often makes the written text of an oral communication seem thin and even tedious. Orality also requires more use of illustrations, comparison, contrast and figurative language to stir the imagination and set up mental pictures in order for the listening ear to take in and process what is being heard.

A case in point is the common historic observation that the communication skills of Thomas Jefferson and Patrick Henry were at the same time both profound and different. Jefferson was seen as a rather ineffective speaker but a brilliant writer whose work remains as some of the most important documents of America's founding. On the other hand, little remains of the transcribed speeches of Patrick Henry, but his oral skills created powerful motivation in his hearers to take drastic and even dangerous steps in responding to his ideas.

Brigance further urges the greater use of questions in order to create a greater dialogic bond between the speaker and the listener. The use of personal elements of address ('you', 'we', 'they') reflect the speaker's need to reckon with the listening audience, while the writer is free to use more impersonal terms because of a primary focus on the subject at hand. Brigance also describes the spoken style that he calls eagerness.[29] It is a quality rooted in the inevitable power of a speaker's passion for the purpose of the speech. The rhythm and tone of the speech express a sense of will and urgency behind the words.

The demands of the acoustical nature of orality are rooted in the reality that speech dies the moment it is uttered. Before the end of a word has been spoken, the beginning of that word no longer exists except in the minds of the speaker and the hearers. A profound issue comes in raising the question whether it is possible to write a manuscript that adequately bridges the diversity between oral and written communication. While I know that my own efforts to succeed in writing orally have usually fallen short, I appeal to the wider experience of homiletical teacher Clyde Fant:

> If today's preaching is not regarded as a lively form of communication, part of the blame at least must be attached to the manuscripted sermon – the art form of homiletics.
>
> This would not be true if the principles for written and oral communication were alike. But they are not. For example, everyone has noticed that even the finest oral communications generally look horrible when transcribed.... What suits the ear does not suit the eye.
>
> What about the corollary of that law? Has it ever occurred to us that if spoken speeches look bad when transcribed, the opposite might also be true – that written speeches sound bad when heard? There are really no exceptions to this law although we've all heard sermons from manuscripts that seem to be. But in those cases, the manuscript has been forced to make radical concessions to the spoken medium.
>
> To overcome these difficulties, teachers of preaching have long advocated 'writing like you speak'. But that is a hybrid art that

nobody teaches. Learning to speak and learning to write are difficult enough in themselves without learning to hybridize the two. And why do it anyway? Why not prepare for the oral medium in the first place?

Preachers should realize that their problems don't stop once they have written a manuscript; in fact, they have just begun – now they really have a problem. What do they *do* with the manuscript?[30]

We will explore the practical aspects of that question later on in the practical issues of preparing the sermon by developing an oral manuscript, an 'oralscript'.

In a similar vein, Fred Craddock reflects on the distinction between orality and literacy when he observes:

> Let a preacher begin thinking that the point is to get Sunday's sermon written, and a string of negative results follow. In the first place, the written sermon is a kind of closure which offers not only a sense of satisfaction – thank God I'm finished with it! – but also a shutting down of germination and gestation, often prematurely.... (T)o make writing the sermon the goal of the process is to cause one to think writing, rather than speaking, throughout the preparation. Preaching is oral communication and to do it most effectively the minister needs to imagine himself or herself, talking with parishioners as the sermon is being formed.
>
> The vast difference between orality and textuality will become apparent as the minister prepares as speaker and not as writer. In textuality, there is more often an overload of information while orality tends to adjust quantity to the brevity and fragility of the communicative moment. Oral presentations cluster ideas and images by association; written presentations arrange ideas and illustrative materials in a linear sequence like words on a page. Writing tends to be more abstract; after all, the reader can double-check and pause for reflection.[31]

Craddock further distinguishes orality from literacy when he observes:

A ... result of making the writing of the sermon one's preparatory goal is that this approach creates for the preacher the very difficult task of getting the message off the page again and into the air. Preparation that moves toward writing must soon thereafter make a radically different move: from writing to speaking.... The very use of a manuscript is spoken of as one would speak of a weakness or of a rule broken, with the tones of confession.... (M)uch of the awkwardness and discontinuity created by writing and then oralizing a text can be relieved by preparing orally from the outset.... Writing as a form of communication has its own integrity, and skills in it should be cultivated. But writing is for reading, and speaking is for listening. Both are, of course, forms of communication, but that kinship is not sufficient ground to argue that one best prepares for the one by doing the other.[32]

In concluding this description of orality and its contrasting nature to literacy, it is important that the case not be overstated. First, orality and literacy should not be seen as antagonists doing combat on the field of communication. All orality in a society that is literate must reckon with the realities of literacy. Even where the unique qualities of orality play the prominent role, we are, at most, a society of secondary orality. The framework of our modern existence is based on the technology that results from literacy. Oral communication must deal with the reality that literacy and literary technology have long held sway in communication. As David Riesman has noted, 'Books are, so to speak, the gunpowder of the mind.'[33] The 'gunpowder' has changed the playing field, but the unchanging nature of the human person still requires that the values of orality be brought to the literate and technological culture. Eric Havelock, in discussing the role of memory in orality, observes the importance of defending this, and by implication, other characteristics of orality:

Educational theorists have often treated memorization as a dirty word, as though all it meant was repetition by rote of material lacking significance. No greater historical mistake could be made.

Our knowledge of ourselves is badly served by such denigration. Not creativity, whatever that may mean, but recall and recollection pose the key to our civilized existence.[34]

The point being raised is that the recall and recollection that shape a society are primarily oral. The foundations of American society that shape a common political body come from such shared recollections. From 'Give me liberty or give me death' to 'Ask not what your country can do for you but ask what can you do for your country' (a statement that while first read from a manuscript entered the human imagination by its oral qualities and rings most powerfully decades later by the rhythm and pattern of orality) to 'I have a dream', oral statements have shaped and united a diverse people to the degree a united society still remains in America. When great thought with its intellectual literary precision fails to move into the oral experience of a people, the sad definition that 'a classic is a book no one reads anymore' becomes the alarming reality.

The goal of this study is that the preacher and those who train preachers have a clear vision of the issues of literacy and orality and how profoundly they impact the preaching task at every juncture. It has been my own experience that failure to appreciate these issues has seriously hindered the effectiveness of preaching. When literacy and orality become blurred in homiletical thought, effectiveness is significantly diminished. Congregations become restless often without knowing why and preachers strain to reach their people. Seminary preparation with its various disciplines needs to play an important role in helping the preacher to develop a working ability to draw from both the written and the spoken elements of communication and to use them to the greatest good.

CHAPTER 3

IS ORALITY A CHRISTIAN CONCERN?

In an era when every trend and novelty has its moment in the sun, is an emphasis on the *spoken* word anything more than a passing interest that will fade away, or is orality deeply embedded in the core of Christian communication? The answer begins to emerge as early as in the third verse of the Bible: 'And God said, "Let there be light"' (Gen. 1:3). From the beginning of its own record, the Christian faith sees the *spoken* word at the root of everything else. Rodney Clapp asserts:

> Ours is the God who did not *write* to create the world, but *spoke* it into being. Our God did not 'inscribe' the Son but 'uttered' him. The Son himself left nothing in writing. He spoke and acted, creating a community of discourse we now call the church. Only there, in life intimately shared, in the close proximity of hearing and touch, is the body of Christ or 'Christianity' really known. Faith, said the apostle Paul, comes by hearing (Rom. 10:17); the (written) letter kills, but the Spirit that enlivens the spoken word lives (2 Cor. 3:6).[1]

Rather than denigrating the Holy Scripture, this observation gives full honor to God's written word by acknowledging that the Bible repeatedly affirms that the *spoken* word stands always behind the *written* word. Eugene Peterson draws this thought further:

> At no place in St. John's Gospel is the word of God simply there – carved in stone, painted on a sign, printed in a book. The word is always *sound*: words spoken and heard, questioned and answered, rejected and obeyed, and, finally, prayed. Christians in the early church were immersed in these conversations and it changed the way they read the Scriptures: Now it was all voice.

They heard Jesus speaking off of every page of the Scriptures. When they preached and taught they did not expound texts, they preached 'Jesus' – a living person with a living voice.[2]

The Hebrew word *dabar* means both 'word' and 'event'.[3] What is most noteworthy about the *dabar* of the Lord is that it is an event unlike all other events. By its very nature an event has its moment in space and time and then it is gone, but the Scripture asserts that 'the word of God stands forever' (Isa. 40:8; 1 Pet. 1:25). The very nature of God's speech is not ephemeral; it is not here today and gone tomorrow. It remains unchanged, undiminished, and unimpeded. It is this word that the Holy Spirit brings to the Holy Scripture.

While it is not within the scope of this project to develop a comprehensive theology of Scripture, it is important to affirm that seeing the intensely oral nature of God's word does not result in diminishing that which the written word claims for itself and that which the Lord Jesus Christ affirms about Scripture. Jesus said that the Scriptures will inevitably be fulfilled and that in the fulfilling of Scripture the smallest details of the written word have the integrity of God's word (Matt. 5:18). At the same time the Lord warned against a misplaced focus on the written word apart from himself, the living word: 'You diligently study the Scriptures, because you think that by them you possess eternal life. These are the Scriptures that testify about me, yet you refuse to come to me to have life' (John 5:39-40).

Perhaps it is not overly simplistic to say that the written word, given by the Holy Spirit to the church (2 Pet. 1:21), provides the people of God with an authoritative, inerrant and fixed record of God's revelatory act which is preserved and enlivened in every generation by the Holy Spirit. This word is to be taken up with grateful humility and faith and preached in the power of the Spirit with an authority that extends only so far as the preaching is faithful to the meaning and purpose of the written text. It is clear that the Bible affirms the importance of both the word of God *written* and *spoken* in accomplishing God's purpose in the world.

This dual expression of God's word suggests important implications in both the nature and function of God making himself known. From our earlier exploration of orality and literacy it has become clear that orality, face to face spoken words, stands at the heart of inter-personal communication. Friends, families and lovers do not regard written communication as the highest and most desirable form of communication. Only when time and distance make face to face communication impossible, does the written word become appropriate. Communication at its foundation is about establishing and maintaining personal relationship and that requires living people in dynamic relationship speaking words to each other. The Bible is replete with this value. God is recorded as having *spoken* to Adam, to Eve, to Cain, to Noah, to Abram, to Rebekah, to Jacob, and to Moses among others in the early part of the Old Testament canon. The prophets are well-remembered as resting their penetrating ministries with the formula, 'This is what the Lord says.' The New Testament writers claim direct and personal communication from God as the basis of what they wrote. In defending his apostolic ministry, Paul asserted, 'I did not receive it from any man, nor was I taught it; rather, I received it by revelation from Jesus Christ' (Gal. 1:12). Peter writes of the foundation of orality when he writes: 'I want you to recall the words spoken in the past by the holy prophets and the command given by our Lord and Savior through your apostles' (2 Pet. 3:2). It is this spoken and personally received message that is committed to written form in the Bible. While the degree of orality may vary, from direct speech to the Holy Spirit's working through the mind and imagination of Spirit-empowered people, living, dynamic and personal communication is clearly the foundation of the Bible. Paul's essential statement, 'All Scripture is God-breathed' (2 Tim. 3:16), affirms the personal and relational nature of God's word to humanity.

From this personal nature of divine communication comes the question, how does reading God's word relate to orality? First, it is clear that the reading of Scripture is, and has always been, an important part of the worship gatherings of God's people. Israel gathered to hear the written word of God read to them (Exod. 24:7; Deut. 31:11; 2 Kgs 23:2; Neh. 8:8; Jer. 36:6; Luke 4:16, 17; Acts 13:27). The New Covenant community as well gave priority to the public reading of God's word, both Old Testament and the apostolic writings (Col. 4:16; Eph. 3:4; 1 Thess. 5:27). A key New Testament statement concerning the receiving of God's word in the congregation is 1 Timothy 4:13: 'Until I come, devote yourself to the public reading of Scripture, to preaching and to teaching.'

Second, it is clear that even the written word was to become oral in the congregation. Scripture was to be *read aloud*. It is a reflection of the depth to which a literate mindset has pervaded our culture that the reason given for such public reading was the high degree of illiteracy in the ancient world. While that may be true, the ancient world recognized that communication, even when written, was not complete in its journey until it was *heard* by the receiver. This is reflected in the account of the Ethiopian eunuch in Acts 8 where Philip *heard* him reading Isaiah the prophet. This common practice of returning the written word to orality, rather than being a concession to illiteracy, reflects a strong consciousness that written communication does not complete its full intended function until it is heard by the people to whom it was addressed. It is the importance of hearing, then, that helps us understand the biblical role of preaching. It is clear that the Bible does expect and emphasize preaching to be an essential component of God's communicating to humanity, both in the congregation of the redeemed and out in the lost world.

Paul's directive to Timothy not only distinguishes the literary from the oral but it establishes the importance of both when he writes, 'Devote yourself to the public reading of Scripture, to preaching and to teaching' (1 Tim. 4:16). Incidentally, it seems that the context in which this was written may suggest that in our own setting we might do well to have our congregations listen to the reading of Scripture without directing them to be looking at the text. While the protest may be heard that some people absorb more from seeing the text than merely by hearing it, there is something to be said for being quiet and extended in mind to take in the word as it is heard. Eugene Peterson makes the bold assertion: 'Reading Scripture is not the same thing as listening to God.'[4] Reflecting themes more fully developed by Jacques Ellul, Peterson suggests that listening and reading are not the same thing. While this line of thinking may at times seem somewhat overstated, common experience tells us that there is an inherent distance and non-relational aspect to reading that must be dealt with. The Bible itself records Jesus' rebuke to his contemporaries that they had an unwarranted confidence in their reading the Scriptures that missed the intent of the God who was speaking to them in those Scriptures: 'You diligently study the Scriptures because you think that by them you possess eternal life. These are the Scriptures that testify about me, yet you refuse to come to me to have life' (John 5:39-40). 'Reading does not, as such, increase our capacity to listen. In some cases it interferes with it.'[5] In reflecting on the nature of reading Peterson observes:

> When I read a book the book does not know if I am paying attention or not; when I listen to a person the person knows very well whether I am paying attention or not. In listening, another initiates the process; when I read I initiate the process. In reading I open the book and attend to the words. I can read by myself; I cannot listen by myself. In listening the speaker is in charge; in reading the reader is in charge.[6]

The cultural tension between an orally oriented community and a literate community comes into practical focus in Peterson's insightful comment:

That hundreds of millions of Bibles are published and distributed is often treated as an immense boon. And it is, but this 'ease of access', when misused becomes a curse. When we read more books, look at more pictures, listen to more music than we can possibly absorb the result of such gluttony is not a cultured mind but a consuming one; what it reads, looks at, listens to, is immediately forgotten, leaving no more traces behind it than yesterday's newspaper.[7]

One of the preacher's primary tasks is to impose personal discipline against this gluttony, to give focused attention to the technologically preserved word and to resist the cultural inclination to allow words to rush by the ear (or the eye) without giving them the hearing that a personal and living word requires in personal inter-relationship. It seems to me that although we tend to think of a carefully prepared sermon manuscript as being very deeply involved with the biblical text the exact opposite may, in fact, be true. It may be that we are transferring linguistic symbols and grammatical structures from the biblical text to the sermon manuscript text without a deep personal hearing that allows the original personal and living word from God to enter the consciousness and imagination of the preacher. If the preacher has not truly heard the living word from the biblical text, it is unlikely that the preacher's listeners will fare any better. Walter Ong, reflects on a cultural phenomenon that has developed from centuries of not only being immersed but also satiated with print:

We are the most abject prisoners of the literate culture in which we have matured. Even with the greatest effort, contemporary man finds it exceedingly difficult, and in many instances quite impossible, to sense what the spoken word actually is. He feels it as a modification of something which normally is or ought to be written.[8]

As was noted concerning Peterson, Ong's assertion may be overstated, but his concern that the person immersed in literacy needs to seek to relate personally to the original writer is both insightful and helpful. The practical issue in this oral-literate tension is that while the most personal and internal part of our personhood seeks the direct and spoken word, our glutted perceptual environment makes focus on the unseen word particularly difficult. The preacher must deal with these dynamics in reflecting on the work of preaching. On the one hand, the person in the congregation wants to receive a personal and living word, but on the other hand, the intensity of visual communication has made the necessary personal focus difficult, if not impossible.

I suggest that it is this very dilemma that makes orality more critical in homiletical thought than it has ever been. A modified or diluted orality that speaks while still being strongly rooted in written thought forms in preparation and with a rather full manuscript or outline will be less effective in saying to the contemporary hearer, 'Listen to me!' The clarity for attraction and focus, for following and involvement, will be less impacting for the hearer and the common complaint of boredom or irrelevance may soon follow. The aphorism 'Paper is a poor conductor of heat' speaks to the problem of the intermediary of the written word still standing in the way of the personal communication that the hearer needs to experience with the living God who speaks.[9] While preaching without notes has a pragmatic value in terms of effectiveness, it at least touches on some of these deeper issues as well.

This brings us to the question of function in communication and it is at this point the importance of the written word comes to the fore. By its very nature pure orality, that is, orality without the aid of technology, exists objectively only in the moment of its utterance. By the time a polysyllabic word is completed, the first part of the word is gone. The air that carried the sound from the mouth of the speaker to the ear of the hearer is already filled with something else. The word now remains only in living memory, first of the speaker and then of the hearer. The endurance of that word as reality that can be known, imagined and acted on is only as strong as the individual or collective memory endures. For that reason, taking the living and spoken word and placing it into the static state of written speech gives an objective and knowable form of the original communication. This written body of communication becomes a foundation, a controlling authority for the community that receives it as the accurate and binding truth of God. The authority of Scripture has been the bedrock for the Church of Jesus Christ from the beginning and the nature of that authority has been at the heart of the debate between the Roman Catholic church and the churches of the Reformation since the sixteenth century. In no way should reflecting on the differences between orality and literacy diminish the historic and essential role of the supremacy of Scripture in the Church. The function of Holy Scripture is essential in Christian orthodox preaching. An untethered flight from the words, definitions, principles, frameworks, stories or visions of Scripture has no place in Christian preaching. Biblical accuracy, care, respect and love for the text are cardinal values for both the Christian church and the Christian preacher.

While affirming this truth without reservation, it is important to note that Scripture itself gives notice that God's word possesses a quality that cannot be reduced to paper and ink. Hebrews 4:12 stands as a fundamental prod to see God's intention to allow Scripture to move from the page to the inner life: 'For the word of God is living and active. Sharper than any double-edged sword, it penetrates even to dividing soul and spirit, joints and marrow; it judges the thoughts and attitudes of the heart.' Clearly, Scripture intends something beyond words on a page in this statement! Psalm 119 is the Bible's great tribute to the beauty and life-giving power that its pages contain. In that psalm the eighteenth verse suggests the need for a personal response to God's word that goes further than eyes seeing written words: 'Open my eyes that I may see wonderful things in your law.' While the allusion here is to seeing, the Scripture more often uses the activity of hearing as the necessary further response to reading. In Revelation two strong assertions complement each other. In concluding John wrote:

I warn everyone who hears the words of the prophecy of this book: If anyone adds anything to them, God will add to him the plagues described in this book. And if anyone takes words away from this book of prophecy, God will take away from him his share in the tree of life and in the holy city, which are described in this book... (Rev. 22:18-19).

Both communication dynamics stand here at the close of the biblical canon: the hearing of God's word which has been emphasized to each of the Asian local churches in chapters two and three: 'He who has an ear, let him hear what the Spirit says to the churches' (Rev. 2:17, 29; 3:13, 22) and the integrity and inviolability of the written word which brings the strongest possible warnings and penalties for either disregarding or tampering with the text of Scripture.

In establishing the distinctions between orality and literacy in God's communication to humanity and affirming the importance of each of them, let us now turn to the implications and meaning of orality for the preacher. Eugene Peterson uses a common pattern to describe the communication process that God has employed to make his message known to humanity: *speaking, writing, reading, listening.*[10] It is the task of every reader of the Bible to press behind the written word to the living God and to press beyond reading to the living voice of God. In the two inner actions of the four phase process – writing and reading – the receiver is in need of the Holy Spirit's help as he or she uses all the mental capacities available to accurately understand and interpret the text. There is no excuse or reason to abandon the disciplines of hermeneutics in seeking to establish the meaning and significance of the biblical text. But no one, private reader or public preacher, has completed God's intended purpose by coming to the point of intellectual accuracy and clarity. Nor is it enough to say that after understanding the historical context and dissecting the grammatical phenomena the reader is now ready to complete the task with some attempts to contextualize the Scripture with application. The 'hearing' spoken of throughout Scripture is far more than that. The further work of orality begins after the accurate message of the text has been established.

Thomas Oden, in describing what he calls his 'reversal' from a critical to a postcritical consciousness in approaching the Scripture, speaks of moving from a filtering mentality by which he meant that he allowed biblical texts to speak to him 'only insofar as they could meet my conditions, my worldview, my assumptions as a modern man'.[11] This became a conflict in him until he came to a critical junction:

> By the middle of the 1970s the idea had gradually begun to dawn upon me with increasing force that it is not my task to create a theology. Newman taught me that the deposit of truth is already sufficiently given, fully and adequately. What I needed to do was to listen. But I could not listen because I found my modern presuppositions constantly tyrannizing my listening.... Then while reading Nemesius something clicked. I realized that I must listen intently, actively, without reservation. Listen in such a way that my whole life depended upon hearing. Listen in such a way that I could see telescopically beyond my modern myopia, to break through the wall of my modern prison, and actually hear voices from the past with different assumptions entirely about the word and time and human culture.... My redirection is in part a hermeneutical reversal by which I learned to listen to premodern texts. But that way of stating it is far too weak, unless one understand that embedded in the deepest idea of listening is obedience (*hupokoa*). I find it difficult to convince colleagues that the most important single lesson I have learned hermeneutically is obedience to the text.[12]

This is where the work of the preacher who desires to hear in order to be able to speak takes up the work. Donald Bloesch relates to the importance of receptive listening when he writes:

> Evangelical Christianity is focused on hearing, not seeing. The kingdom of God is not a visible reality but an invisible one that makes its way in the world through the proclamation of the gospel

(cf. Luke 17:20-21).... Because the true God is incomprehensible and invisible, because he transcends all sight and understanding, he cannot be made known until he makes himself known. And God has made himself known fully and decisively in this one person, Jesus Christ.... We make contact with Christ only through hearing the gospel about Christ, which we encounter in the Bible and also in the proclamation and ministration of the church (cf. Rom. 10:14-17; 1 Cor. 1:21). Luther observed, 'In order to see God we must learn to put our eyes into our ears.'[13]

In starkly graphic but deeply biblical language, Thomas Oden reflects on the ancient church's insight into the relationship between the virginal conception of Christ and spiritual receptivity of all Christians:

The bodily locus of the virginal conception was not portrayed in early Christian art as the vagina, but the ear: *'The conception was by hearing'*, as distinguished from the birth, which, 'was by the usual orifice through which children are born, even though there are some who concoct an idle tale of His being born from the side of the Mother of God' (John of Damascus...). In early iconography the Holy Spirit is not portrayed as coming into Mary's body physiologically by sexual transmission, but spiritually by attentive hearing. The birth was by 'the usual orifice', the uterine canal; but the conception was by right hearing of the Word of God. Accordingly, Mary remains in Christian memory the primary prototype of human readiness to receive God's coming (Julian of Norwich...).[14]

The psalmist expresses this when he writes, 'Today, if you hear his voice, do not harden your hearts as you did...' (Psa. 95:7). The point of all this is simply to establish that orality is far more than just a matter of delivery technique. Even if the preacher chooses to preach with the use of a manuscript, the essential power of the sermon is found in the preacher's having deeply heard the word of God in the reading of the biblical text. 'Hearing without hardening' may be one of the most important aspects of preparation in the preaching of God's word.

Closely related to hearing God's word is the human response of prayer. I believe it is not too much to say that prayer finds its full place in the theology of preaching when we consider orality as the essence of preaching. Jacques Ellul puts it succinctly: 'God speaks. We must answer him.'[15] If, in fact, we regard the Scripture as the very word of God given to us, then we must not only give ourselves to a deep hearing of his word, but we must honor his initiative in speaking to us by responding and speaking to him in prayer. I suggest that one of the key aspects of the orality of preaching is that the preacher conveys to the congregation not only the accurate transmission of the text's meaning but also reflects the deep hearing and responding to the text that brings personal insight, new vision from the Lord's message and submissive response. This personal inter-action with the text begins to change the categories and structures of communication from the primarily literate, with its accurate specificity and detailed and intricate thought, to a more broadly conceived frame of reference that, while more penetrating, is less detailed and while very pointed in its concern, is more imagery oriented than is the specificity of a verbal concept. Orality in preaching is the result of a deep hearing of God's word, a thorough personal response to God's word (a response that can largely be seen as the answering of prayer), and a speaking of the resulting message to a congregation that is consistent with this highly personal experience with the written word.

The importance of orality in our present cultural context becomes more apparent as we are seeing an increased demand for imagery in Christian worship gatherings, both in high and low church settings. The historic high church focus on liturgy with its highly visual drama is now being met in the low church setting with an equal emphasis on imagery through technology and life situation dramatic pieces. Often the use of technological imagery is an attempt to create a bridge to secular culture through the use of visual images. This 'seeker sensitive' emphasis on the visual is done with the explanation that in a visual and media age these techniques are essential in reaching the secular unchurched person. Without considering the broader issues of the context in which pre-evangelism and proclamation evangelism is best done, it can be said that the predominance of visual imagery in both high and low church practice raises profound theological issues. Jacques Ellul writes extensively about the importance of distinguishing between the impact of image and the impact of the word. He draws heavily on the story of the temptation and fall of humanity in Genesis 3:

> I see. What I see is evident and certain. It gives evidence against the Word. This is the real 'temptation', and the process by which we question truth. Rather than remaining in a fluid relationship based on listening, word, memory, choice, and response, the woman sees a possible way to take possession and to dominate at the level of this reality that she recognizes as the only stable one. She *hears* the true word placed in doubt. These two facts are closely related, and based on them the opposition to images is made explicit, as the irreconcilable contradiction of image and word is ascertained.[16]

Throughout his discussion, Ellul speaks of the pressing weight of the impact of imagery over against the 'weaker' more free-giving influence of the word, where the listener has much more inner space and necessity to take in, evaluate and decide how to respond to the word that has been heard. Implicit in this is the greater weakness of the word, of the relative uncertainty of the response the word will elicit in comparison to the compelling power of image alone. Advertising has made much of this in our culture. The skillful use of image comes much closer to guaranteeing the result the originator intended than the word itself will be likely to accomplish. Words leave more room for a person to choose a variety of responses than good sales technique wishes to accommodate. Therefore, the humble power of the mere word is set aside in order to attain more certain results. And that is just the problem. Ellul, referring to Eve, writes:

This is the first time sight is a separate issue. This sight refers to the tree of the knowledge *of good and evil*; that is to say, the tree of discernment of the truth. She sees; she no longer hears a word to know what is good, bad, or true. She sees – reality. She sees the *reality* of this tree. What she sees has no relationship with the word – neither with the serpent's word nor later with her own word, and finally not with Adam's word when he speaks to God.[17]

The task of the preacher is to take up the word of God as it is given in the biblical text and to express it clearly to the listeners, not just in a mere verbatim repetition of the written word, but with a hearing and responding spirit that takes the word laid to rest in the fixity of written language and returns it by the power of both the human spirit and the Spirit of God to penetrate the inner ear of the listeners. This transaction, from the written text, to the inner life of the preacher, to the speaking context of the listener, is at the core of the oral experience. This is why the Bible itself has urgent imperatives that the written word of God must be preached. The crisis to which the preacher speaks is a world of people whose imaginations are inflamed by sight, by the immediate, by what Ellul calls 'reality', but it is a 'reality' unmarked and unjudged by the authoritative, albeit 'humble' word of God. The word must be returned to the forefront of the listeners' minds and imaginations. God's definitive commands, his contrasting atmosphere of what is good, true and right, must be spoken into the hearing of the world, so that the mere impact of visual images does not dominate the entire range of our thoughts and values. When this kind of speaking goes forth, it is the essence of orality. It is what Paul referred to when he wrote, 'By setting forth the truth plainly we commend ourselves to every man's conscience in the sight of God' (2 Cor. 4:2). This dynamic encounter of the person of the preacher with the conscience of the listener seems to stand at the core of biblical preaching. While being rooted deeply in the words of the written text, the outer relationships are being re-established by the process of *speaking-writing-reading-listening*. The preacher who has listened in the fullest sense, including all the disciplines of the hermeneutical process, who has meditated on the text, has been impacted so as to pray back in response to God what this text has done in his own life, is ready to stand before a gathering of hearers and preach in the apostolic manner: 'Our gospel came to you not simply with words, but also with power, and the Holy Spirit and with deep conviction' (1 Thess. 1:5).

It is this personal and spiritual dynamic that stands at the heart of orality. Delivery style should be seen not merely as a technical matter of pragmatic effectiveness but as an intrinsic extension of the very purpose behind the command 'Preach the word' (2 Tim. 4:2).

The foregoing discussion of the purpose and manner of preaching from a biblical and theological perspective raises the question why, then, is so little attention given to the form and delivery of the sermon in mainstream theological studies? Clyde Fant proposes that the answer may be found in the divorce between theology and practical homiletics among preachers and seminary faculties:

> For all the prominence accorded the *theory* of preaching by theology, the *practice* of preaching has not enjoyed equal attention. The *what* of preaching is frequently regarded as concern enough; the *how* of preaching is merely a matter of rhetoric: 'The renewal of our proclamation means that there remains only a question of what we proclaim, not the question of how we proclaim it.' There are two reasons for this. First, homiletics is frequently regarded as a branch of rhetoric rather than of theology; and second, some theologians do not believe that preaching can be taught at all – which really means that the *what* of preaching can be taught, but the *how* of preaching cannot.
>
> An example of this first point of view is to be found in Gustaf Wingren's book *The Living Word*, an excellent inquiry into 'the essential nature of preaching'. Wingren asserts, however, that 'such very practical questions as the construction of the sermon, its delivery and such like obviously do not fall within our field. Homiletics as a part of practical theology has its own specific

problems *which are not theological in nature'*. In other words, homiletics is indeed a division of practical theology, but the practical questions of preaching, such as the construction of the sermon and its delivery, *are not theological in nature.*[18]

Fant pleads for the uniting of the theoretical and practical aspects of homiletics:

If we do not do so, then preaching as a practical act within the church will be hopelessly schizoid. One half of its personality will be Hebrew-Christian, and the other half will be Greek-pagan. Perhaps the theoretical idea of preaching, or even the content of the sermon itself, may be solidly theological and Christian; but the *actual* sermon, the *preached* sermon, which cannot avoid its essential entanglement with questions of form, methodology, and delivery, will be weakly rhetorical and pagan. We will have 'severed the head of preaching from theology and dropped it into the basket of rhetoric held by Aristotle'.[19]

While there is a danger in trying to claim too much for matters of structure and style in preaching, Fant clearly describes a great deal of the reason why issues of orality have played only marginal roles on the periphery of homiletical thought and why issues of delivery have seemed somewhat less than worthy of serious focus and consideration as theological issues themselves. In fact, a considerable amount of the homiletical discussion relative to orality seems more closely tied to the practical and pragmatic than to the biblical and theological concerns that have been presented above.

Robin Meyers observes:

Perhaps the single biggest failure in the teaching of preaching is that young ministers are not fully impressed with the difference between textuality and orality. Shaped by mountains of books, called upon to write scores of papers, and graded largely by what they commit to the page, aspiring preachers train the eye but neglect the ear. Yet it is into the world of sound that they will go, plying their wares acoustically. The major elements of public ministry (the sermon, the funeral eulogy, the marriage ceremony) are all rhetorical moments. No one will see their outlines, much less grade them. Rather, as Jesus warned, 'By their *words* they will be justified, by their *words* they will be condemned.'[20]

Frederick Buechner expresses the spiritual urgency of the preaching moment:

In the front pews the old ladies turn up their hearing aids, and a young lady slips her six-year-old a Life Saver and a Magic Marker. A college sophomore home for vacation who is there because he was dragged there, slumps forward with his chin in his hand. The vice-president of a bank who twice this week has considered suicide places his hymnal in the rack. A pregnant girl feels the life stir inside her. A high school teacher, who for twenty years has managed to keep his homosexuality a secret for the most part even from himself, creases his order of service down the center with his thumbnail and tucks it under his knee.... The preacher pulls the little cord that turns on the lectern light and deals out his note cards like a river boat gambler. The stakes have never been higher. Two minutes from now he may have lost his listeners completely to their own thoughts, but at this moment he has them in the palm of his hand. The silence in the shabby church is deafening because everybody is listening to it.... Everybody knows the kinds of things he has told them before and not told them, but who knows what this time, out of the silence, he will tell them.[21]

At such a moment, an occurrence in every church everywhere every Sunday, it does not seem to be a time to read to people. This is a moment for talk – direct talk, engaging talk, talk that goes from the core of the preacher and seeks to be allowed entry to the core of the hearer. Such a situation needs the full weight of both theological and practical understanding joined together in unity.

How then, has the common practice of significant dependence on written notes and manuscripts come to be so prevalent among preachers? Apart from the highly literary disciplines of ministerial training (biblical languages, theology, church history) the very study of great oral preachers has been reduced to a literary experience. Clyde Fant has touched on one fascinating explanation:

> Following the nineteenth century and the advent of popular literacy, the sermon was steadily transformed from its original oral medium into a literary, written medium. This change was partly due to the impact of printing as a medium for communication and partly due to the sensational success of the 'comets in the Gutenberg galaxy' – to play with McLuhan's term – the literary preachers to that literary age.
>
> The influence of these preachers upon the form of the modern sermon is incalculable. The sermons of Robertson, Spurgeon, and others were printed and distributed to millions. Homileticians subsequently used those written sermons as models of excellence for their preaching classes. And although this approach unquestionably produced many good results, it also had one unfortunate effect upon the sermon. Students were encouraged, directly or indirectly, to *write* sermons like the ones they were reading.
>
> As a result, the sermon was increasingly prepared for the eye rather than the ear. Devices suited for reading – paragraphing, formal syntax, tightly fitted logical arguments, complex outlines, literary language – were superimposed upon the sermon. Of course the sermon continued to be delivered orally, but increasingly from a manuscript really prepared for reading.[22]

Fant could well have mentioned that many of these great sermons were first preached orally, with all the freedom and vitality that orality creates, and only later were reduced to writing and edited to remove much of the situational and dialogical quality of the sermon as it was actually preached and to add literary structures such as paragraphing and linguistic precision that may not have been part of the heard sermon at all. I can well remember, in fact, reading the sermons of Spurgeon as a young ministerial student and becoming restless over the lack of organization and depth. I have now come to understand that this restlessness was a reaction to reading sermons in which the editing for print had diluted the quality of orality. Since that time, I have found that *reading* Spurgeon with an attempt to *hear* Spurgeon is a far more satisfactory exercise. It seems to recapture the impact that his preaching had on those who actually heard him.

While the focus in this part of the project is on biblical and theological implications of orality, much of what has been said so far could be put under the Greek rhetorical classification of pathos, the personal and relational importance of the message being embodied in the person who is speaking. This personal dynamic creates several important values.

Immediacy, the sense of a vital and important personal interchange, is essential in biblical preaching. Craig Loscalzo quotes a laywoman who was invited to address a doctor of ministry seminar. She said, 'I don't want a sermon read to me. If the preacher has to read to me, just give me the manuscript and I'll take it home and read it myself.'[23] She was quickly affirmed by other lay people in the group. In a relationally distressed age, people coming to hear the word of God have a hunger for a deep sense of the immediate and the personal. Eugene Peterson quotes Ezra Pound's H. Selwyn Mauberly expressing this thirst for directness: 'Tell it to me, all of it, I guzzle with outstretched ears!'[24] While typical churchgoers may not wish to be so openly passionate, the hunger to hear deeply from the heart of one person to their own inner lives is a river that runs deep in them. Richard Ward writes of the preacher as a prism and recognizes that any preacher desiring effectiveness longs for a greater degree of transparency, a strong and perceptible unity between *who* the preacher is, *what* the preacher says, and *how* the preacher says it. He reflects on the low place homiletical studies have given 'delivery':

> Many books on the art of preaching wait until later to introduce the old character named 'Delivery'; he is not usually consulted until all talk of composing the sermon is done and the preacher is impatiently concerned with how to speak what she has written.

'Delivery' (who comes from a distinguished family known as 'Rhetoric') often takes the stage in the final chapter and is only allowed to speak about technique-stylistic devices such as enunciation, pitch, gesture, and volume.... Rhetoric is more concerned about stimulating the speaker's creativity and imagination than about 'polishing' her 'style' or 'ornament'. If we listen to Rhetoric on his own turf, we will see that he does not begin with how the speaker sounds (diction) but who the speaker is (ethos). 'The character (ethos) of the speaker is a cause for persuasion when the speech is so uttered as to make him worthy of belief....'

In order to speak well, the preacher must first be honest with him or herself, be able to take a hard look at how he or she gets any piece of work done, and then learn to 'develop areas of (the) personality that in the past have been suppressed.... The process of becoming a more credible speaker begins with looking and listening: to the deep interiorities of self, to the chorus of voices assembled in texts, and to the cries of the community.[25]

Ward relates these values of immediacy and personal connectedness to the very core of the preacher and the preaching act:

We are all part of a culture which values quick results. Preachers have become consumers of those methods which will help them get results faster and more efficiently. As a result, many preachers do not give themselves time for original thought. These preachers are tempted to become copies of someone else. They have usually been taught to devalue their own experiences or at least are not given meaningful clues about how to incorporate those experiences into their ministry of preaching. Because they do not know how to approach the question of origins, many preachers become more imitative than creative.[26]

I suspect that this dependence on the highly developed literary thoughts and styles of others has something to do with an almost instinctual retreat from the values and practice of an oral style of preaching. Different preachers must identify and discipline their own weaknesses, whether they be overly given to careless study of a biblical text or lack of confidence to internalize the message of a text through their own personality and experience. The kind of preaching that gives hearers a sense that they are hearing a person speak with the authenticity of having stood in the presence of God requires an openness and transparency that freely flows from the mouth and life of one preacher standing alone before a gathering of people. In a letter to Billy Graham, Helmut Thielicke wrote, 'It is indeed a part of the style of the fellowship willed by God that it not be mediated by printer's ink, but rather requires physical nearness and directness.'[27] That is the inner demand of orality.

The Lewises cite several leading homileticians on this matter of immediacy. George Buttrick is cited as claiming, 'In most churches a manuscript even dramatically read would be a barrier between preacher and people.' And Henry Ward Beecher is claimed to have said, 'A written sermon is apt to reach out like a gloved hand, an unwritten sermon reaches out the warm and glowing palm, bare to the touch.'[28] My own experience in preaching in a more oral style has brought many comments such as 'You seem to be preaching more from your heart'. I confess that such comments are somewhat frustrating because I have *always* sought to preach from my heart. The problem seems to have been that a style deeply rooted in literacy failed to convey what I was feeling.

Bert Decker, a modern business communications specialist, draws heavily on the importance of not assuming that what we feel is what the listeners perceive. He relates the experience of a preacher who for twenty years had been tied to his pulpit and his notes. One Sunday, convinced it was time to get free and to move away from the pulpit, he chose to use a moment to tell a story at the end of the sermon to do so. He was terrified. He felt forced and artificial, but he did it anyway. He saw himself at great risk and leaving behind his sources of security. His congregation saw exactly the opposite. They saw their pastor come near and stand among them as a living person who was talking directly with them without a barrier. Decker cites this experience as an example of an important communication principle: 'There is a *big* difference between the way we see and experience our own performance and the way others see us.'[29] Getting free and becoming natural (and perhaps in the process discovering what 'natural' is!) is a great gift to our hearers, even when initially it is costly to the preacher.

Within the concerns of immediacy is the commonly affirmed importance of eye contact between the preacher and the listeners. Orality cuts to the core of this important communication dynamic by giving the speaker fewer places to look! The spiritual importance of direct and personal communication is greatly heightened by the freedom of the preacher to look at the congregation. Even the psychological tendencies to look away because of nervousness or fear are reduced because the mental and emotional framework is to talk to these people. The only exception to making eye contact now is looking at the Bible in hand. That change of visual focus has its own positive message for the congregation.

Another value that will require more discussion later on is the issue of *retention*. 'Remember!' is one of the great words of the Christian faith. Both Old and New Testaments are filled with the injunction to recall the history, the teaching, the promises, and the commands that are part of the heritage. Above all, the Christian is commanded to remember Jesus Christ. In an information age, where most of what we *may need to know* is conveniently available and can be looked up without great effort, the preacher needs to keep the vision of giving the congregation not only what *can* be recalled by going to a continually available source but what *is actively before* the listener as a word retained from hearing God's word preached. The Lord emphasized the importance of the retentive quality of the word in the parable of the four soils. Luke records the essential trilogy of response to God's word: 'But the seed on good soil stands for those with a noble and good heart, who *hear* the word, *retain* it, and by *persevering* produce a crop'

(Luke 8:15). It was this issue of retention that forced me to first examine my lack of orality in preaching. When a magazine editor (a rather literate person!) told me she could only remember about 20% of what I preached, I began to think more carefully about orality. There is an entire craft and discipline to memorable preaching that deserves its own space, but for the moment it is important simply to establish the value of retention in preaching.

Retention has two dimensions. The preacher must be able to remember what it is he wishes to say. To be sure, the preacher is in the advantaged position since hours of preparation have been devoted to the sermon. If anyone should remember the sermon, the preacher should! I find it startling to admit that I have occasionally asked preaching colleagues to recall what they have just recently preached only to discover they are unable to remember. As for the congregations of such preachers, statistics may be too cruel to explore. If the preacher had to go into the pulpit with written material to help recall the sermon and if the congregation is seated without benefit of notes or manuscript, it is unlikely much of that sermon will leave the room. Of course, there is the possibility of either taking notes or having notes provided, but then the act of preaching has become more an act of learning the content of a lecture (an entirely appropriate activity since it concerns the Bible and the Kingdom of God), but the act of listening to the preaching of God's word as it addresses the heart, mind and will is diluted. Richard Eslinger contrasts 'talking about' and 'speaking of' that touch on the importance of using language that is highly imaged and is shaped with a sense of urgency. He is referring to the quality of abstraction, which is a common quality of literacy, over against the more earthy and colorful language of orality. He writes:

> Lacking such language, congregations simply tune out the preacher's words; the intended message slips unnoticed from their awareness.

All too often, our preaching employs a kind of speech ('talk about') that, predictably so, is extremely difficult to be heard and retained. Such speech simply cannot form in congregational consciousness. Preaching from within this homiletical pit of 'talk about' results in sermons that largely cannot be retained by the hearers. (Estimates of retention are as low as 25 percent of the language spoken.)[30]

While literacy may tend to abstraction and orality to concreteness, there is no guarantee that one of necessity is linked to the other. In fact, thought that has resulted from labour with paper and pen may serve the concrete nature of earthy description as a preparation for orality, while unthoughtful orality may tend to soar to unfocused abstraction more easily than literate communication. The point to be taken is that orality maximizes the potential for personal and living description that engages not only the mind but the imagination of the hearer.

Another biblical dynamic of preaching is *dialogue*, or what Barbara Bate calls interdependence.[31] In the story of Peter's sermon at Pentecost, it seems that while what Peter said was filled with significant theological and experiential truth, something beyond Peter himself was going on. Luke tells us that 'Peter stood up with the Eleven, raised his voice and addressed the crowd' (Acts 2:14). Clearly the preaching event was far more than carefully prepared material that Peter conveyed to his hearers. The Holy Spirit's presence was an integral part of the event for all concerned. The Eleven stood with Peter as he preached and their confirming presence impacted both Peter and the gathering. The work of the Spirit upon the gathering certainly was a shaping and motivating power in Peter as he preached. Toward the end of the sermon the dialogic power of the event was so strong that the people actually spoke and asked, not just Peter but the apostolic group, 'Brothers, what shall we do?' (Acts 2:37). Paul implies this interdependence as a crucial part of the church's life even when he is not physically present, but someone else is speaking the word of God. In directing the Corinthian church to take disciplinary action toward a sinning member, he tells them, 'When you are assembled in the name of our Lord Jesus and I am with you in spirit, and the power of our Lord Jesus is present, hand this man over to Satan....' (1 Cor. 5:4) While the text does not make direct reference to preaching *per se*, the clear intent of the apostle is to describe the atmosphere in which the word of God is to be spoken and acted on in the Christian assembly. The presence and working of the Holy Spirit in each constituent part of the gathering is an important dynamic in the life of the church. Orality creates the optimal possibility for the preacher to be aware of and give himself to all that the Spirit is doing in the entire preaching context. In that openness, the preacher maximizes the role of the Holy Spirit in the entire preaching event. This quality of dialogue is most commonly experienced in the Afro-American congregational setting. Anyone who has preached with the dynamic of congregational involvement knows the power of it. While less overt gradations of that dialogue may be more in keeping with the culture of many congregations, whenever the preacher and the congregation are communicating clearly with each other, the power of the message soars.

Persuasion also stands as a critical factor in orality. While the preacher has the responsibility to teach and inform, the primary task is to urge the congregation to respond to God's word in appropriate action. The preacher targets the inactivity in the heart, mind, and life of his hearers. Ruskin described a sermon as 'thirty minutes to raise the dead'.[32] Jowett urged:

And in all our preaching we must preach for verdicts. We must present our case, we must seek a verdict, and we must ask for immediate execution of the verdict. We are not in the pulpit to please the fancy. We are not there even to inform the mind, or to disturb the emotions, or to sway the judgment. These are only preparatives along the journey. Our ultimate object is to move the will, to set it in another course, to increase its pace, and to make it sing 'in the ways of God's commandments'.[33]

Richard Storrs, a Brooklyn preacher, gave a series of lectures at Union Theological Seminary in 1875 on conditions of success in preaching without notes. He referred to his previous experience in training for the legal profession:

> All these men, of course, were in the habit of speaking constantly, without notes, before the full Bench, or to the Jury; in the most important and difficult cases, as well as in those of lighter consequence; when arguing difficult questions of law, as well as when discussing an issue of facts. I never knew but one lawyer who was in the habit of reading his arguments from a full manuscript; and he, though an able, was a remarkably timid man, whose argument was always addressed to the Judge, not to the jury.
>
> I could not see, therefore, why a minister – however limited in faculty and in culture, in comparison certainly with these eminent men – should not do that before his congregation, which lawyers were doing all the time in the courts; and when my plans of life were changed, under the impulse as I thought of God's Spirit, and I had devoted myself to the ministry, I determined if possible to fit myself to do this, and to preach without reading. It seemed to me that this was the more apostolic way, at least. I could not learn that Paul had pulled out a Greek manuscript, and undertook to read it with his infirm eyes, when he addressed the woman at Philippi; or even when he spoke on Mars Hill, under the shadow of the Propylea and the Parthenon, to the critical Athenians. It seemed to me that to speak to men without notes, out of a full and earnest mind, was now as then the most natural and effective way to address them.[34]

The communication values of the lawyer seeking to persuade the jury hold strong ties to the concerns of the preacher who is preaching to move people to give themselves to the call of God in Christ Jesus. Macleod recalls Fosdick's tireless question:

> 'What do I propose to do this morning?' That meant: What conviction does the preacher wish to convince his hearers of before God? Will the contagion of the sermon emerge with the impact of the Pauline: 'This one thing I know ... I believe ... I do'?[35]

One last quality of orality in preaching that is clearly within the biblical and theological framework is *indeterminacy*. Indeterminacy is that quality of preaching where the sermon 'cannot be a finished product before it is heard; its hearing and application are decided in various ways by those present in worship'.[36] While closely related to the dialogical nature of preaching, indeterminacy stands on its own as a biblical and practical issue in Christian preaching. From the beginning of the Bible to the end, even within the literary framework of the written word, most of the preaching recorded in Scripture reflects far more than preachers standing behind pulpits and speaking from written supporting notes. Rather, these servants of the word stood before their people and proclaimed God's word from the depth of their being. From Moses, to the prophets, to the Lord himself and to the apostles, preaching that was deeply rooted in Scripture and in the present situation came forth in free and existential expression at the moment of speaking.

Clyde Fant speaks of the evanescent quality of preaching as being well suited and even essential for revealing God to us:

> Preaching, then, appears weak because it disappears into the experience of others; it vanishes, seemingly without a trace: 'Language seeks to disappear; it seeks to die as an object.' But this is precisely what makes preaching essential to the Christian faith. It shares a great mystery with the incarnation, 'Word become flesh', and 'eternal Word become subjective words.' So preaching avoids the idolatry of fixation, the static representation of God by objects, however apt or beautiful. So preaching allows participation by the hearer, interpretation, and appropriation. It is taken up in every generation by every individual who proclaims, not as an object but as subject. It is therefore, *open*, not closed; *I* may participate in this reality. 'From its trajectory of death, resurrection and return, this story has a forward orientation; it is open to the future, and it is precisely its incompleteness which makes our participation possible.'[37]

It is important that these words not be extended into the arena of revealed truth in Scripture. There is a fixity of truth in Scripture, a body of theological conviction that has served the Church for centuries as orthodoxy, but the act of preaching at its best always rises to touch the lower edges of the unchanging word. Orality conveys that reality well.

Thomas Long reflects on the evanescence of preaching when he writes:

> A 'written' sermon is a contradiction in terms. Of course, many sermons are written down *before* they are preached, and some sermons are written up *after* they are preached, but a sermon itself occurs not in the writing but in the preaching. A sermon, by definition, is a spoken event. This is an important distinction, since speaking and writing are not merely two separate but equal channels of communication. The effects of the spoken word are markedly different from those of the written word.[38]

While the indeterminacy of oral preaching may create a sense of incompleteness and even anxiety for the preacher prior to the preaching event, that very sense is part of the authenticity of preaching. In the 1905 Yale lectures R. W. Dale quoted his predecessor John Angell James on finding security in reading the sermon:

> If I preach without reading I shall be miserable for three weeks – miserable until I am in the pulpit; if I read, I shall be quite happy till I begin to preach, though I shall be miserable till I finish.[39]

That honest and humorous admission often stands at the heart of the preacher's resistance of coming to terms with the reality that preaching has an evanescent quality that a written pulpit resource only serves to obscure. Any preacher who speaks to more than one Sunday morning service with the same sermon knows that what seemed to bring life to the first congregation must have a new and personal investment in preaching for the later congregation to experience some of that same grace.

Orality is not merely an attractive technique to draw the attention and approval of a contemporary congregation with its heightened expectations and needs. Orality in preaching touches the core of Christian biblical and theological values.

CHAPTER 4

A HISTORY OF ORALITY IN PREACHING

Because many preachers seem to fear oral practice in preaching and some actively oppose it, a brief survey of the orality of preaching in practice and thought is an important part of the discussion. A comment by Daniel Baumann suggests that the oral approach to preaching is merely a respected but seldom achieved ideal:

> Although preaching without notes is enthusiastically commended by many theorists, it does not find much acceptance on the part of practitioners. A recent study of preaching within one denomination revealed that less than one in twenty use this method.[1]

Concerning opposition to oral practice in preaching, we find a fierce spokesman in the writing of Karl Barth (1886-1968), a man who started a world-wide theological revolution as a local church pastor:

> Many great themes emerge in the preaching of Barth. The first of these regards preaching and the sacraments. Barth regarded preaching as the *oral* form of the communication of the gospel; the *visible* form was the sacraments. He believed that 'a complete evangelical service ought to begin with baptism, continue with preaching, and end with the Holy Supper'. As preaching is a witnessed revelation in word, the sacrament is a witness in picture.[2]

Yet in spite of the emphasis Barth placed on the existential orality word of God, he was passionate about the necessity of sermons being carefully prepared and delivered from completely written manuscripts:

> The basic prerequisite in execution is to write the sermon. This condition is so important that a thorough argument in its favor

seems to be needed. To be sure, a sermon is a speech. It has to be this. But in this speech we should not leave it up to the Holy Spirit (or some other spirit!) to inspire the words, no matter whether we have an aptitude for speaking or not. Instead, a sermon is a speech which we have prepared word for word and written down. This alone accords with its dignity. If it is true in general that we must give an account of every idle word, we must do so especially in our preaching.... Each sermon should be ready for print, as it were, before it is delivered.[3]

Barth's passion for taking seriously the preaching of God's word and the necessity of careful preparation gave no place for an oral approach to preaching.

In a survey of the Yale lectures on preaching Baxter notes:

Twenty-two of the Yale lectures discussed the relative desirability of the three most widely used methods of delivering the sermon: reading from manuscript, speaking from memory, and extemporaneous preaching. The broadest difference of opinion in the entire series of lectures occurred on this question.[4]

After reviewing the lectures from 1871-1944 Baxter concluded:

Just as the manufacturer knows that, no matter how excellent his product, there are no profits until after delivery, so the thoughtful preacher knows that, no matter how fine the sermon, there is no profit until after the sermon is actually delivered to the minds and hearts of the people. Successful delivery is not universal. Only after long years of constant attention and continued practice does one achieve the art of delivering sermons effectively....

... the method of delivery which is most widely used by successful preachers is the extemporaneous method. This method means neither that there has been no preparation of the sermon, nor that the preparation has been sketchy and haphazard. The extemporaneous sermon is best when it has been preceded by the written sermon. Rather than read from the manuscript, the extemporaneous preacher leaves it at his desk, delivering his message with eye and body as well as with his voice.[5]

Most of the preaching I have heard has been by preachers using rather extensive notes. My own seminary training hardly referred to the issues of orality at all, and until beginning to delve into this project I had encountered few homiletical textbooks that gave specific instruction on the methodology of note-free preaching. Most of the effective note-free preaching I have heard was done by itinerant preachers who have the freedom to develop a limited number of sermons and repeat them frequently. It was in the doctoral seminars taught by David Larsen that I first encountered both a credible model and the beginnings of a methodology of orality. The seed was planted that led me to investigate orality and the issue of note-free preaching as a serious issue in my own preaching. This further directed me to investigate the role of orality in the history of preaching.

Thomas Long relates one of the great issues of preaching in this delightful description:

Once upon a time, homiletics (the theological study of preaching) and rhetoric (the art of effective speaking) were a happily married couple. From Augustine's *On Christian Doctrine* (perhaps the earliest homiletical treatise in Christian literature) all the way to the big, systematic homiletical textbooks in vogue in the nineteenth century, Christian homiletics looked to the Bible and to theology for the *content* of sermons and then to the rules and fashions of classical rhetoric for the *form* and *style* of sermons. It was a mixed marriage – homiletics being Jewish and rabbinical in background, and thus religious; rhetoric being Greek, gentile, and ideologically neutral – and it was a marriage of convenience, but it worked well. Homileticians knew what preachers were supposed to say, and rhetoricians knew how they were to say it, so that listeners could hear it and be persuaded by it. On some occasions theological homiletics took the lead role in the marriage, and on other occasions rhetoric was the governing force, but working together, aiming to 'be fruitful and multiply', homiletics and rhetoric set out to produce sermons that were both faithful to the gospel and adapted to the capacities of the hearers.[6]

Long traces the 'at times' uneasy marriage of these disciplines until he comes to the present, and claims that biblical truth has always been set forth in the context of the ongoing conversation of the church and the world. While theological homiletics is foundational, the study of communication principles needs to come alongside in order to keep preaching from falling into abstract ideas that give no practical direction.

R. Paul Stevens understands the sermon as we know it today:

> The sermon in the sense of a twenty-five minute message constructed in a formal way for maximum persuasive effect, is an art form that arose in the Christian West from a combination of Hebrew prophecy, Greek rhetoric, Jewish synagogue preaching, and the impact of the Christian gospel (Dargon 1:14). Originally the Latin word *sermo* meant 'dialogue' because early Christian instruction involved interaction with hearers.[7]

Fred Craddock also asserts:

> There is no form that can be identified as 'sermon'. Of course, those persons who have listened to the same type of sermon for many years think they know what a sermon form is. They may even assume that seminaries uniformly instruct the students to shape their messages in that fashion; after all, a sermon is a sermon. However, there is no evidence that the Jewish or Christian communities created an oral form and called it a sermon. In preparing written materials, the church adopted with appropriate modifications available forms such as the epistle, the apocalypse, and perhaps even patterned the Gospel form after that of biographies of heroes. Likewise, Greek rhetoric was employed as a form for proclamation of the gospel. Even though that rhetoric dominated the field of homiletics for centuries, not even that pattern of oral presentations can justifiably be called *the* form of a sermon. It remains to this day that a sermon is defined more by content and purpose than by form.[8]

It is the limited purpose of this chapter to trace orality through some of the more prominent and easily identifiable movements and figures in the history of the Church. Paul Scott Wilson places the preaching of the infant church squarely in the oral form with the assertion that there was in the first century Jewish community a prohibition against writing. Concerning the ultimate development of the Mishnah (a Hebrew commentary on the Jewish Law) and the Targum (a translation of the Scriptures into Aramaic) he writes:

> Both of these oral projects were committed to memory, for to use writing was to place them on an equal footing with 'That Which Was Written'. (Scholars in Jerusalem were regretting this had happened, three centuries earlier, in Alexandria with the translation of the Torah into the Greek Septuagint.) It was many years before this prohibition against writing was dropped. In time, the writing of the oral accounts of Jesus, within the Jewish ethos in particular, was acknowledgment of the divine status and authority given to Jesus' words and acts.[9]

While several critical perspectives could be formed from that historical context, there is little question that orality was the predominant preaching value in the early church's origin. In his extended article on 'History of Preaching' Edwards suggests:

> In the strict terms of the definition, there are probably no sermons as such in the New Testament, no texts that had been delivered orally to an assembly for evangelization, instruction, or worship. There seems to be little reason to think that the shape of Christian preaching in the New Testament period can be reconstructed.[10]

Even with that disclaimer concerning actual sermonic models in the New Testament, it is not difficult to agree with Ralph Lewis' assertion:

> The reading of speeches was rare among the Greeks and Romans. While we regard Paul's epistles as written sermons for the early church intended to be read by whatever congregation he was addressing, there is no indication Paul ever read a sermon to any of his congregations.

It is difficult, if not impossible to picture Jesus reading the Sermon on the Mount, or His parables of the good Samaritan, the lost coin, the lost sheep, or the prodigal son, just as it is hard to imagine Paul reading his sermon to the philosophers on Mars Hill, or Peter unrolling a scroll on the day of Pentecost to read the divine summons to repent and believe.[11]

Edwards credits Origen (ca. 185-253) for the creation of what we have come to identify as the classical form of the homily. 'Origen stood to deliver these homilies extemporaneously after he had prepared himself exegetically, and they were taken down by a stenographer.'[12]

John Chrysostom (ca. 347-407), one of the most revered figures of the Eastern Church, most likely preached without notes. His sermons were recorded by stenographers and written out afterward for publication.[13]

Sometimes his congregation would erupt into applause for the beauty and power of his speech, but he would quickly remind them that their praise meant nothing unless they put into practice what he was urging them to do. For his sole aim was the spiritual and moral growth of his listeners; as he would say to them, 'If I see you living in piety, I have all I wish.'[14]

Augustine (354-430) stands at the foundation of the great Western tradition of the Church:

Augustine's sermons were recorded by secretaries on the spot. Unlike the bishop's books, his sermons exist today in their original unrevised form: exegetical pieces expressed in a homiletic medium of everyday speech. On occasion their extemporaneous character was tested to the limit when the lector read the wrong psalm and the bishop graciously accommodated himself to the mistake.

The Basilica of Peace at Hippo measured a mere 126 feet (with apse, 147 feet) in length, and 60 feet in width, comparable in size to many rural churches. Still Augustine sometimes bemoaned that his voice could not be heard above the muttering crowd, except in complete silence. His remarkable conversational style –

reminiscent of the Cynic diatribe and rife with questions directed toward his listeners. His fondness for anaphora, antithesis, and alliteration frequently elicited vocal response and applause.[15]

Fant and Pinson speak of his oral method:

As for his technique, Augustine seems to have composed his sermons by careful mental preparation, committed the major points to memory, and left the details and examples to be recalled at the moment of delivery. He watched his audience closely and altered his sermon according to their response. He once said that if the audience was tired, he finished quickly.[16]

Lewis observes:

A shift took place before the end of the fourth century. By A.D. 400 most Christian preaching had absorbed the principles of Greek rhetoric. In the centuries since, most preachers trained in rhetorical studies have abandoned the simple structure popular in the New Testament church for the more formal structure of the learned Greek model. The logical intricacy and the rhetorical structures of these deductive arguments are not as easy to remember without the prompting of written notes.[17]

The great mystic Bernard of Clairvaux (1090-1153) seems to have continued in the heritage of orality.

We do know that it was his custom to meditate on his sermon in his cell or in a rustic arbor. Then he usually preached with little or no reference to notes; in fact, there is much evidence that he spoke extemporaneously. In one of his sermons Bernard says, 'Another sense also occurs to me, which I had not thought of before, but which I must pass over.' From such a comment it is obvious that Bernard did not read from a manuscript. He added material as it occurred to him. No doubt he worked from a structure, but he altered that structure as suited his mood or the occasion. This freedom in delivery appealed to the common man.[18]

When we arrive at the medieval theologian Thomas Aquinas, we do not find a model for sermonic delivery.

During his canonization process one witness stated that he watched Thomas preach through the whole of Lent with his eyes closed or ecstatically turned toward heaven. There was little of classical oratory about him. Nor did he use a violent manner, dramatic gestures, or flashing wit.

Did Thomas preach from the meager sermon notes which remain? No one can answer with certainty. On the one hand, he is said to have had a prodigious memory; yet his own biographer says that he did not learn any more languages because of his absent-mindedness. Could the great intellect have spoken extemporaneously from such bare skeletons, clothing his thoughts in appropriate language?

On the other hand, we might well imagine the meticulous scholar preaching from a complete manuscript. These homilies may only be fragments which remain of larger works. At any rate, the issue appears lost in antiquity, and we will have to content ourselves with wondering.[19]

Coming to Martin Luther, we encounter a preacher who was amazing in the sheer volume of sermons that he preached. Gritsch estimates that Luther preached between 4,000 and 10,000 times; 2,300 sermons are extant, the bulk of them recorded by listeners rather than by his own hand.[20] Edwards describes his method:

Beginning with the medieval thematic sermons, he went on to develop a form that was unique. It resembles that of patristic homilies but concentrates not so much on individual verses as what he considered to be the 'center of meaning', the 'heart point', or the 'kernel' of the passage. Having identified that, he would develop an outline that would enable him to get the point across. Yet he did not prepare by writing out a manuscript; instead, he immersed himself in the text and then preached extemporaneously, beginning with a statement of the *Herzpunkt* and going from there to extract that meaning from his text. In the pulpit he would have no more than a brief outline of what he meant to say, his *Konzept*, but he departed from that often enough for someone to say that the structure of his sermons was one of 'heroic disorder'.... Since he considered preaching to be an eschatological struggle in which Christ would elect individuals and save them from the enemy, his preaching was powerful.[21]

John Calvin (1509-1564) might be thought to be a dry and scholarly preacher lost in his manuscript, but that is not the case. Fant and Pinson's description of him states:

(He) was an excellent preacher who spoke entirely without manuscript and frequently without specific preparation. The very criticisms we might imagine of Calvin – cold, dull, lost-in-his-manuscript, pedantic – are entirely unjustified. He did speak slowly and deliberately, but always extemporaneously and directly. His preaching was logical, but never without underlying power and confidence. On the other hand, the virtues we imagine – the careful study, the meticulous argument – are the very points at which he has been most severely criticized. Many of his sermons were delivered entirely without preparation – and they reflect it. But we must remember that Calvin preached almost daily over a number of years; and although his general study continued without interruption, specific preparation on any one sermon was frequently absent.[22]

The great Scottish preacher John Knox (1513-1572) 'prepared himself by careful study to expound the passage of Scripture selected for his text, then trusted to his feelings at the time for the mode of expression which he might use in delivery'.[23]

In England, a change took place in the midst of religious turmoil:

The use of complete manuscripts were not introduced into the pulpit until the 16th or 17th century. Manuscripts were popularized in the English establishment as a backlash against the Independents and the Puritans, whose impassioned preaching scandalized and scared royalty and clergy alike. Anything approaching extemporaneous preaching met with such official disfavor that one cleric was driven from his London pulpit because he lifted his eyes from his manuscript and looked at his congregation like the Dissenters did when they preached.[24]

John Broadus identifies the introduction of the sermon manuscript as occurring during the reign of Henry VIII. Quoting Burnet, Broadus says:

Those who were licensed to preach ... being often accused for their sermons, and complaints being made to the King by hot men on both sides, they came generally to write and read their sermons, and thence the reading of sermons grew into a practice in this church.[25]

Commenting on the French Catholic preacher Jacques Bossuet (1627-1704), Fant and Pinson pay tribute to the biblical character of his preaching and remark of his delivery:

Apparently he often spoke with scant preparation, so that few of his sermons were put on paper before being delivered. Bossuet was not alone in that: one of the most surprising conclusions from a careful study of the notable preachers from every century is that many of them did only oral or mental composition before they spoke.[26]

Although not as highly regarded for his preaching as for his writing, Francois Fenelon (1651-1715) is remembered for his thoughts on orality cited in his *Dialogues on Eloquence:*

A man who is well instructed and who has a great facility of expressing himself; a man who has meditated deeply in all their bearings upon the principles of the subject which he is to treat; who has conceived that subject in his intellect, and arranged his arguments in the clearest manner, who has prepared a certain number of striking figures and of touching sentiments which may render it sensible and bring it home to his hearers; who knows perfectly all that he ought to say, and the precise place in which to say it, so that nothing remains at the moment of delivery but to find words to express himself – such is the extempore speaker.[27]

Ralph and Gregg Lewis raise the issue of the spiritual power expressed in orality in the question:

> Could it be merely coincidence that the greatest revivals and church growth have usually occurred in periods of history when extemporaneous preaching was a vital aspect of the religious scene? The great evangelical awakening grew out of the vigorous extemporaneous styles of men like the Wesleys, Whitefield, Fletcher, Coke, Nelson and others like them.
>
> Despite the testimony of testing and history, some ministers cling to the manuscript habit with the argument that a written sermon will have lasting value. Yet, the enduring qualities of sermon manuscripts are of little or no consequence to most congregations or preachers. Who reads printed sermons of past centuries or even recent decades? Only seminary classes in preaching. A few preachers read sermon magazines. But who else? Almost no one *reads* sermons; but millions *hear* them every week.... If we're concerned about the permanence of a particular sermon, we might do well to follow the advice of Augustine who suggested writing out sermons only after they were preached.[28]

With these strong affirmations of orality we turn to the preaching of the English speaking world. In Edwards' article on the history of preaching, he discusses the Elocutionary Movement and its interest on delivery:

> It grew in part out of a conviction that one of the reasons the Methodists were drawing members away from the established church was the liveliness of their delivery in comparison to 'the cold, artificial manner' with which so many clergy read their notes from the pulpit. (Hogarth's prints depict the deadliness of the one and the extravagance of the other.)[29]

One of the most significant questions concerning the orality of preaching might be Jonathan Edwards (1703-1758) and his famous sermon 'Sinners in the Hands of an Angry God'. Reports of Edwards reading this sermon commonly follow the description given by Fant and Pinson:

> The sermon exploded like a bombshell in the congregation. This is all the more remarkable when we remember that Edwards was frail and sickly, his voice thin and weak, his eyesight dim. He preached with a full manuscript held closely before his eyes, his manner almost passive, devoid of gestures.[30]

Edwards' biographer Iain Murray questions the accuracy of this account and suggests an alternative view:

> What probably happened was that Edwards for some twenty years took his full manuscript into the pulpit. He never read it word for word and he gradually became less dependent on it. Then, for an intermediate period, he continued to write at some length but took only a brief skeleton – 'thumb papers' as the East Windsor people called them – into the pulpit with him. Finally, he ceased to write in full and prepared only an extended outline. That the Great Awakening period coincided with this change is not without interest. It is not that he simply became too busy to write his sermons fully. Rather he was now more fully convinced, as Grandfather Stoddard had been long before, that freedom from dependence on a manuscript was in best accord with the true nature of preaching. His former attachment to notes, says Hopkins, he came to regard as a 'defect and infirmity'. He was inclined to think it had been better if he had never accustomed himself to use his notes at all.[31]

Closely involved with Edwards was the English preacher George Whitefield (1714-1770).

> Whitefield preached without a manuscript. He spent long hours in the study preparing his sermons, and at times he did attempt to use a manuscript; but Whitefield felt that he was at his best preaching freely to an audience. Because of the success of his unorthodox style of delivery, Whitefield reformed the habits of as many preachers in the pulpit as he did laymen in the pews.[32]

An additional observation concerning the transcription and editing of Whitefield's sermons concerns an important issue in the study of preaching:

> In the case of Whitefield – as in the case of many great preachers of the past – many false impressions of his preaching have been given by the poor editing of his sermons. Sometimes these editions have become obsolete with the passing of years; but in other collections of Whitefield's sermons, his racy, natural prose has suffered 'polishing' of the sorriest sort.
>
> For example, read his sermon 'the Burning Bush'; then read 'Walking with God'. Do they sound like the same preacher? They do not. 'The Burning Bush' was stenographically recorded and reproduced exactly as Whitefield spoke it; the other sermon has been edited out of its style by someone who was obviously embarrassed by Whitefield's roughness. Some editions of Whitefield's works make him sound cold and intellectually sterile. Whitefield himself wouldn't recognize his sermons in that form. No doubt many interpreters of Christian preaching have been deceived by such miserable alterations of what was once great preaching.[33]

Timothy Dwight (1752-1817), grandson of Jonathan Edwards and president of Yale University, stood as a tower of strength against the currents of atheism in young America.

Because Dwight suffered from poor eyesight, he found it virtually impossible to write his sermons in full. As a result he had to deliver most of them extemporaneously. In the long run this proved to be a great advantage to him – not to be tied to a manuscript, as were most preachers of that era. Once during a revival Dwight preached a sermon which he had written out fully, but he became so excited toward the end of his sermon that he added an extemporaneous conclusion. One gentleman in the congregation later asked permission to see the manuscript, explaining that he wanted to read the conclusion because he considered it the most elegant he had ever heard. To his surprise he discovered that the conclusion was the only part of the sermon not carefully composed in advance.

It had been created under the inspiration of the moment.

His method of sermon preparation was simple. During the week he went over each sermon in his mind during 'free moments' – such as hoeing his garden, riding his horse to call on parishioners, or visiting the sick. By the end of the week he had written nothing, but he had the material for his sermon completely planned and organized. By Sunday his two sermons were ready. An hour before the service he jotted down a brief outline of the principle points he wanted to make. Even this step required only a few moments because he wrote quickly and in an abbreviated shorthand. The entire sermon could be contained on a quarter sheet of paper which he held in his hand. Occasionally Dwight referred to his outline, but he usually relied on the inspiration of the moment for the development of the sermon. Those who heard him reported that he never hesitated, was never at a loss for words, and usually preached for an hour.[34]

The famous Scottish preacher Robert Murray McCheyne (1813-1843), who died at the age of 29, was remembered by his biographer as one who came to strong orality in his preaching:

From the very beginning of his ministry, he reprobated the custom of reading sermons, believing that to do so does exceedingly weaken the freedom and natural fervor of the messenger in delivering his message. Neither did he recite what he had written. But his custom was to impress on his memory the substance of what he had beforehand carefully written, and then to speak as he found liberty. One morning, as he rode rapidly along to Dunipace, his written sermons were dropped on the wayside. This accident prevented him having the opportunity of preparing in his usual manner; but he was enabled to preach with more than usual freedom. For the first time in his life, he discovered that he possessed the gift of extemporaneous composition, and learned, to his own surprise, that he had more composedness of mind and command of language than he had believed. This discovery, however, did not in the least degree diminish his diligent preparation.[35]

Frederick W. Robertson (1816-1853), was another highly honored English preacher who died at an early age. He described his sermonic method to his bishop:

The word *extempore* does not exactly describe the way I preach. I first make copious notes; then draw out a form (rough plan); afterwards write copiously, sometimes twice or thrice, the thoughts, to disentangle them and arrange them into a connected whole; then I make a syllabus, and lastly, a skeleton which I take into the pulpit.[36]

Robertson depended upon the clarity of his arrangement to aid him in delivery. He planned his divisions and kept to them from the beginning to the end of his sermon without using the few notes he carried with him. Sometimes he would even crumple in his hand the sheet of rough notes he carried with him into the pulpit. Robertson's mind was full of his subject and he spoke out of his thorough preparation; but he never relied entirely on his prodigious memory.[37]

Robertson once wrote in a letter:

Now, without method memory is useless. Detached facts are practically valueless. All public speakers know the value of method. Persons not accustomed to it imagine that a speech is learnt by heart. Knowing a little about the matter, I will venture to say that if anyone attempted that plan, either he must have a marvelous memory, or else he would break down three times out of five. It simply depends upon correct arrangement. The words and sentences are left to the moment; the thoughts methodised beforehand: and the words, if the thoughts are rightly arranged, will place themselves.[38]

On January 13, 20, 27, 1875, the Brooklyn preacher Richard Storrs gave a series of lectures on preaching at Union Theological Seminary in New York City. As a student of the legal profession he was deeply impressed by the power of lawyers who argued their cases without referring to notes. Storrs related his own experience of having to communicate to a

congregation with an enormous diversity of intellectual powers
and spiritual interests. He spoke with imagery that has often
been repeated by other advocates of orality:

> It was simply idle to try to hold the attention of an audience so
> various, promiscuous, and untrained as that, while reading from a
> manuscript. Numbers of them would have laughed in my face,
> and have left the house. Certainly they would never have come a
> second time. Inserting a manuscript between them and myself,
> would have been like cutting the telegraph-wires, and putting a
> sheet of paper into the gap. See if you then can send your message
> on the wire! The electricity would not pass.[39]

Cox summarizes Storrs' method:

> Rewriting the outline of the sermon again and again – twenty
> times if necessary – until each successive point of movement of
> thought would be present before the preacher when needed as the
> sermon is preached. This rewriting is not a copying from page to
> page; it is a true rewriting, in which the preacher recreates the
> ideas, perhaps in different words, each time the outline is rewritten.
> In this way, the preacher will not struggle from point to point, but
> will be freely carried along with the flow of thought.[40]

Other than Spurgeon perhaps no preacher has had more of
his sermons published than Alexander Maclaren (1826-1910),
yet Maclaren never wrote manuscripts of his sermons. He
preached entirely without notes:

> I began my ministry with the resolution that I would not write my
> sermons, *but would think and feel them*, and I have stuck to it ever
> since. It costs quite as much time in preparation as writing, and a
> far greater expenditure of nervous energy in delivery, but I am
> sure that it is best for me, and equally sure that everybody has to
> find his own way.
>
> I write my sermons in part. The amount of written matter varies.
> When I can, I like to write a couple of sentences or so of
> introduction, in order to get a fair start, and for the rest I content

myself with jottings, fragmentary hints of a word or two each, interspersed here and there with a fully written sentence. Illustrations and metaphors, I never write; a word suffices for them. If I have *heads*, I word these carefully and I like to write the closing sentences. I do not adhere to what is written, as there is very little of it that is sufficiently consecutive. I make no attempt to reproduce more than the general course of thought and constantly find that the best bits of my sermon make themselves in preaching. *I do adhere to* my *introductory* sentences, which serve to shove me off into deep water; beyond that I let the moment shape the thing. Expression I do not prepare; if I can get the fire alight, that is what I care for most. This is my ideal, a sufficiently scrappy one you will think, but I am frequently obliged to preach with much less preparation. The amount written varies from about six or seven pages of ordinary note paper to the barest skeleton that would go in half a page.[41]

John A. Broadus (1827-1895) is best known for his preaching textbook, *On the Preparation and Delivery of Sermons*, possibly the most widely used text in the history of preaching. What is less known is that Broadus was also an outstanding preacher himself. Cox writes of preachers who 'like Broadus, prefer to use their available time in production of the ideas of the sermon'.[42]

Broadus was a meticulous scholar and he left two large notebooks filled with the dates, places, and texts of all the sermons preached during his whole life. But he did not preach from a manuscript. He spoke extemporaneously, and many critics reported that the printed page was a poor substitute for the experience of actually hearing Broadus himself.... It is unfortunate, however, that the extemporaneous style of Broadus did not leave us with more manuscripts.[43]

Joseph Parker (1830-1902), whose fame grew as pastor of London's City Temple, lived in an era of tremendously prominent preachers in London. He found his experience with overdependence on manuscripts to be a major detriment in his delivery.

> Early in his ministry he wrote out his sermons in full, but later he became impatient with the method. He was not successful when he preached from a full manuscript; Nicoll said that the only time that Parker failed miserably in his preaching was on an occasion when he read a sermon before the Union of Churches in Scotland, a sermon which he had prepared for months and written out with meticulous revision. In his London lectures on preaching, *Ad Clerum*, delivered early in his career, he advised young ministers to write out their sermons for the first five to seven years.... In those lectures he urged his students to write and rewrite their sermons; nevertheless, he vigorously opposed their reading from manuscripts. He urged them to 'preach the gospel rather than read it'. Parker believed in careful preparation and study, even to the point of oral preparation; but when the moment came to preach he did not depend upon any manuscript or notes but spoke freely, drawing inspiration from the moment.[44]

Charles Haddon Spurgeon (1834-1892) preached in London to what was then the largest regular congregation in the world. His following was global and even today over two hundred publications written or edited by him are still in print.

> Spurgeon never wrote manuscripts of his sermons before they were preached. In fact, it has been said that he never 'touched pen to paper' during the entire preparation of his sermon. Perhaps that was frequently or even usually true, but the existence of sermon outlines denies that it was invariably true. In reading his sermons today, it seems incredible that such incomparable diction and precise prose could have been orally composed.
>
> Nevertheless, he was unquestionably a genius in delivery. Read any page of his sermons — remember that they were stenographically recorded — and imagine the impact of such words delivered without the hindrance of notes or manuscript. Spurgeon's oral style may have been the finest ever produced by the Christian pulpit.[45]

Included in Spurgeon's widely noted book, *Lectures to My Students*, is a talk he gave on 'The Faculty of Impromptu Speech':

> Very strongly do I warn all of you against reading your sermons, but I recommend, as a most healthful exercise, and as a great aid towards attaining extemporising power, the frequent writing of them. Those of us who write a great deal in other forms, for the press, etc., may not so much require that exercise; but if you do not use the pen in other ways, you will be wise to write at least some of your sermons, and revise them with great care. Leave them at home afterwards, but still write them out, that you may be preserved from a slipshod style.[46]

By this writing discipline, however, he did not mean that he thought memorizing written material a wise preaching method.

> We do not recommend the plan of learning sermons by heart, and repeating them from memory; that is both a wearisome exercise of an inferior power of the mind and an indolent neglect of other and superior faculties. The most arduous and commendable plan is to store your mind with matter upon the subject of discourse, and then to deliver yourself with appropriate words which suggest themselves at the time. This is not extemporaneous preaching; the words are extempore, as I think they always should be, but the thoughts are the result of research and study. Only thoughtless persons think this to be easy; it is at once the most laborious and the most efficient mode of preaching.[47]

Spurgeon compared the work of the preacher to that of the attorney in the courtroom:

> But the gentlemen of the bar are many of them most ready speakers, and as you will clearly see, they must to a considerable degree be extemporaneous speakers too, because it would be impossible for them always to foresee the line of argument which the evidence, or the temper of the judge, or the pleadings of the other side would require. However well a case may be prepared,

points must and will arise requiring an active mind and a fluent tongue to deal with them. Indeed, I have been astonished to observe the witty, sharp, and in every way appropriate replies which counsel will throw off without forethought in our courts of law. What a barrister can do in advocating the cause of his client, you and I should surely be able to do in the cause of God. The bar must not be allowed to excel the pulpit. We will be as expert in intellectual arms as any men, be they who they may, God helping us.[48]

Spurgeon taught his students that it is important to be diligent in maintaining the ability of impromptu speech.

If you are happy enough to acquire the power of extemporary speech, pray recollect that *you may very readily lose it*. I have been very struck with this in my own experience, and I refer to that because it is the best evidence that I can give you. If for two successive Sundays I make my notes a little longer and fuller than usual, I find on the third occasion that I require them longer still; and I also observe that if on occasions I lean a little more to my recollection of my thoughts, and am not so extemporaneous as I have been accustomed to be, there is a direct craving and even an increased necessity for pre-composition. If a man begins to walk with a stick merely for a whim, he will soon come to *require* a stick; if you indulge your eyes with spectacles they will speedily demand them as a permanent appendage.... Ill uses create an ill nature. You must continually practise extemporising, and if to gain suitable opportunities you should frequently speak the word in cottages, in the school-rooms of our hamlets, or to two or three by the wayside, your profiting shall be known unto all men.[49]

In 1911 David James Burrell, pastor of Marble Collegiate Church in New York City, gave the inaugural Sprunt Lectures at Union Theological Seminary in Virginia. In his lecture on method of delivery Burrell spoke of the importance of the preacher's freedom in preaching:

Hilariter is a good word for the pulpit. Freely, joyously, without the hindrance of the least self-consciousness, leaning hopefully on an almighty arm, filled with the enthusiasm of the divinely-struck moment, thrilled through and through with the life-giving truth of his message and longing to make every hearer see it as he sees it – so should the preacher preach. Therefore, whatever his mode of preparation and delivery, he should above all things trust God and let go![50]

Burrell quoted several thoughtful sources concerning the importance of free delivery, such as the words of Joseph Parker:

For many years I have been unable to agree with my brethren whom I do not regard as preachers at all. From my point of view they were vigorous readers of admirable essays, but they had no right or title to be regarded as preachers. In my judgment there is all the difference in the world between reading and preaching. The reader stands at a distance from the hearer; the preacher goes down to the hearer and talks to him directly, and, as it were, personally. The reader may be reading something six months or six years old, whereas the preacher speaks to the immediate moment and the immediate environment.[51]

Drawing from the *Edinburgh Review* for 1802 Burrell gave this observation:

Pulpit discourses have insensibly dwindled from speaking to reading; a practice of itself sufficient to stifle every germ of eloquence. It is only by the fresh feelings of the heart that mankind can be very powerfully affected. What can be more ludicrous than an orator delivering stale indignation, and fervour of a week old; turning over whole pages of violent passions written out.[52]

Burrell gave the following methodology for preaching without notes but only after full preparation:

1. Have something to say. An essayist may have a message or note, as he pleases; but a paperless preacher will fail utterly unless he has something to say.
2. Prepare faithfully. The man who supposes that he can satisfy an audience of thinking people with an improvisation is a poor

student of human nature and deserves to fail.... Do not memorize the manuscript. The important matter is to know precisely what one wants to say. We have a truth to demonstrate; let us demonstrate it. We have a moral precept to enforce; let us enforce it. We have a path to pursue; let us pursue it.

3. Forget yourself. The great advantage of the unread sermon is that it permits an absolute abandon. The manuscript is not only a non-conductor between the speaker and his audience, it is a grave objection to preaching *memoriter*; the effort to remember is a diversion. When the preacher rises to his task, nothing should stand between him and the matter at hand.... Let yourself go! Run with your message! You have done your best in honest preparation; now trust in God.

4. Don't be discouraged by failure.... In any case let us, as ministers, remember that we are not our own but God's men, not doing our own but God's work. Wherefore 'if any man speak, let him speak as the oracles of God; if any man minister, let him do it as of the ability which God giveth; that God in all things may be glorified through Jesus Christ, to whom be praise and dominion forever and ever'.[53]

In pleading for preaching without written support Burrell charges preachers: 'Let us get back again to the root of *sermon*; it is "a thrust"; a thrust with the sword of the Spirit, which is the Word of God.'[54]

Charles Brown (1862-1950) held pastorates across the United States, twice gave the Lyman Beecher Lectures on Preaching and was Dean of the Yale Divinity School. He was named one of the twenty-five most influential preachers in America in 1924. Brown began preaching with a total dependence on a written manuscript but came to believe that he was not communicating with his congregation and took up the practice of preaching without any dependence on notes. He relates his agony in launching out without his written supports:

When I broke away from that method and undertook to learn to preach without a manuscript, I was beaten with rods of mortification. Again and again I suffered shipwreck. By day and by night I have been in the deep, right in my own pulpit. I floundered around for many a bad half hour where I knew the water was over my head and was painfully aware of the fact that I had not learned to swim.

In weariness and in painfulness, with backache on Sunday night and headache on Monday morning, in cold chills and in mental nakedness, I have labored at it because I believed that the spoken word could be made more effective than the word read from the manuscript.... I am here to say that almost any man, *almost* any man, can learn to do it, if he is willing to pay the price.[55]

Brown's confidence did not come easily and he described his initiation. The first time he preached free of his notes he lasted only eleven minutes and had nothing left to say. When his church leaders, fearing he was ill asked about his health, he confessed what had happened to a lawyer in his congregation who said:

Keep right on! Keep right on, Parson – we would rather have eleven minutes of that sort of preaching than half an hour of the other. I would never risk one of my cases in court by taking in a carefully prepared manuscript to be read to the jury. You are pleading for a verdict and for a much more important verdict than it is ever my lot to secure. Keep your eyes on the jury and talk right at them.[56]

While taking care to write out and memorize a few sentences for the introduction and conclusion, Brown preached without a manuscript for the rest of his ministry.[57]

G. Campbell Morgan (1863-1945) was rejected by the Methodist Church as a young man whose trial sermon showed no promise for preaching. At the end of his life he was being invited to begin a pastorate at the age of 72. He was one of the most prominent preachers in both England and America in the first half of the twentieth century.

Then sometimes I am asked about methods of delivery. Well, all I can say, is as a rule, I have a brief. I never prepare sentences. I do not know when I rise to preach what my first sentence will be as to form. I know what the thing I want to say is. I speak from a brief most carefully prepared, and I give myself freedom of utterance.[58]

George Truett (1867-1944) served the First Baptist Church of Dallas, Texas, for almost fifty years and built that church into one of the largest congregations in the world. Fant and Pinson report:

Those who heard Truett preach have insisted for years that his printed sermons reveal nothing of the power of the man. It has become a cliché among Southern Baptists that Truett was one of the most exciting preachers to hear and one of the most disappointing to read. Since Truett preached without manuscript, it has been generally assumed that he was simply another example of a man who was a master of oral style, but whose printed sermons read poorly. That same complaint has been registered countless times about many preachers, most of whom have been dead so long that no recorded sermons could possibly have existed.

But Truett's situation presents a different case; hundreds of his sermons have been preserved on records and tape. Examination of those tapes reveals a startling conclusion: Truett's sermons were so revised in editing that much of his distinctive style was removed. If his sermons had been printed exactly as they were delivered, a different preacher might have emerged from the page.[59]

Arthur John Gossip (1873-1954) is best known for the classic sermon he preached after the death of his wife, 'But When Life Tumbles In, What Then?' His sermon delivery was described by the Principal of Trinity College, Glasgow:

Often he gave the impression that his preaching was wholly spontaneous, the inspired utterance of the occasion, as the Spirit of God led him on; but the truth probably was that he had taken to himself the counsel which he gave in his *Warrack Lectures* to his students, that the wisest method in sermon-making is that man first should write 'In order that things may not be vague or unwieldy or disorderly', and then should commit it substantially to memory, for, he adds shrewdly, 'If a discourse is too elaborate and subtle to be delivered without manuscript, it is certainly too subtle and elaborate to be followed without a paper before the hearers too' ... the prevailing impression made by his preaching was that of a vital personality charged with communication of a vital and urgent message. That message was clothed in pithy and ardent words which reached the heart and played upon the feelings, a revivifying of energy and resurgence of hope.[60]

Harry Emerson Fosdick (1878-1969) has been called the father of modern preaching. This towering figure who stood against the fundamentalists in the theological controversies that marked America in the first half of the twentieth century, drew both opponents and admirers to hear him preach.

He used three methods of delivery in his preaching ministry: memorization, extemporaneous preaching, and manuscript reading. He used the first method early in his first pastorate, but it took too much time; so he changed to extemporaneous preaching, by which he meant that he completely wrote out his message and then spoke from a brief outline. He used this method for most of his ministry, but he finally changed to reading the sermon late in his career. Even then he continued to speak freely. Fosdick believed that a sermon should be delivered conversationally but with vigor and enthusiasm.[61]

Joseph Fort Newton (1878-1950) traveled widely in his pastorates, from First Baptist Church of Paris, Texas, to The City Temple in London. He began as a Southern Baptist, became a Universalist and ended his ministry as an Episcopalian priest.

In homiletical thinking Newton was just as revolutionary. He did not believe in writing out a full manuscript, nor preaching from one as his style of oratory might suggest. In fact, one of the reasons for his fame was his ability to speak classic sentences of poetic style, abundantly illustrated from literature, without the use of notes. He wrote his sermons only after they were delivered. He was not intoxicated with words; he believed that style amounted to more than well-turned phrases.[62]

Clarence Macartney (1879-1957) was a prominent Presbyterian preacher in the first half of the twentieth century who stood against liberalism in his denomination and was contrasted prominently over against Harry Emerson Fosdick. His preaching delivery became most widely known through his book, *Preaching Without Notes*.[63] Oddly enough, while Macartney emphasized a strong and logical outline as the key to being able to recall the sermon, Fant and Pinson fault the erratic nature of his development and credit the ability of his listeners to follow his sermons to his descriptive powers.[64]

William Temple (1881-1944) has been called the most renowned Primate in the Church of England since the English Revolution. During the last two years of his life he was the Archbishop of Canterbury. A preacher of great intellectual power, 'He did not use a manuscript; if he carried anything at all into the pulpit with him, it would only be a small half sheet of notepaper with a few headings on it'.[65]

The first great television preacher was the Catholic bishop Fulton J. Sheen (1895-1976). During the infant days of television his weekly twenty-three minute sermons received the highest popularity ratings ever recorded for an inspirational or intellectual program. He preached completely without notes.

It was Sheen's custom to think through his sermons during the week prior to broadcast, gathering material and carefully structuring his ideas – but he did not write a manuscript, much to the mutual fascination and fright of television officials. Sheen correctly recognized the need for spontaneity in a program of that sort and flatly refused to run the risk of appearing stiff and unnatural by being tied to a manuscript. In the preface to his book of sermons, *Life is Worth Living*, taken from his television broadcasts, he wrote: 'Our telecasts were given without notes of any kind, nor were they written out prior to appearing before the camera.'[66]

Norman Vincent Peale (1899-1993) became one of the most popular American preachers of the twentieth century. While many regard his theology as Neo-Pelagian, he insisted always that he was deeply committed to the historic reformed faith.

His sermons are short, averaging about twenty-five minutes in length of delivery. Peale lays great stress on understanding the personality of the audience; he believes that every group of listeners has it own mood, and that the speaker must shape his message to meet its particular needs. He believes that a speaker can literally radiate love out across a congregation until he has enveloped them in a feeling of good will.

Peale always speaks extemporaneously. He believes that reading or memorizing a sermon blocks spontaneity and interferes with the audience empathy. He believes in leaving the exact expression to the inspiration of the moment.[67]

Describing her husband's preaching, Mrs. Peale wrote:

I have never known Dr. Peale to write a manuscript for his sermons, but he always prepares an outline. Usually it consists of an introduction and three points, which are put down in such a way that he has freedom of selection as he speaks. Depending on how much time he devotes to the first section, he decides as he is preaching whether to use all three points or only two, and which point he will eliminate.

It has never ceased to amaze me that Dr. Peale always delivers his sermons without notes of any kind, and that both sermons are as nearly identical as it is possible to make them. He never takes his outline into the pulpit; nor does he memorize it. Instead he photographs it on his mind in such a way that he can visualize clearly its point-by-point progression as he speaks.[68]

No contrast could seem greater than the preaching world of Norman Vincent Peale and Martyn Lloyd-Jones (1899-1981), yet in the manner of sermon delivery both shared a respect for the importance of orality. In his teaching on preaching Lloyd-Jones seemed reluctant to regard technique or craft as having any part of this holy task. Yet in his theology there is to be found a concern for delivery. Sargent writes, 'One cannot separate Lloyd-Jones's pneumatology from his homiletics.'[69]

Lloyd-Jones spoke of the 'act' of preaching:

> Though the sermon has been prepared in the way we have indicated, and prepared carefully, yet the preacher must be free in the act of preaching, in the delivery of the sermon. He must not be too tied to his preparation and by it. This is a crucial point; this is of the very essence of this act of preaching. I am not thinking merely in terms of having a manuscript with him in the pulpit, for he can be tied without having a manuscript. All I am saying is that he must be free; free in the sense that he must be open to the inspiration of the moment. Regarding preaching as I do as an activity of the Holy Spirit, we have to emphasize this point because the preparation is not finished just when a man has finished his preparation of his sermon. One of the remarkable things about preaching is that often one finds that the best things one says are things that have not been premeditated, and were not even thought of in the preparation of the sermon, but are given while one is actually speaking and preaching.
>
> Another element to which I attach importance is that the preacher while speaking should in a sense be deriving something from his congregation. There are those present in the congregation who are spiritually-minded people, and filled with the Spirit, and they make their contribution to the occasion. There is always an element of exchange in true preaching. This is another way of showing the vital distinction between an essay and a lecture on the one hand, and a preached sermon on the other hand. The man who reads his essay gets nothing from his audience, he has it all there before him in what he has written; there is nothing new or creative taking place, no exchange. But the preacher – he has prepared, and prepared carefully – because of this element of spiritual freedom is still able to receive something from the congregation, and does so. There is an interplay, action and response, and this often makes a very vital difference.[70]

William Sangster (1900-1960), prominent British Methodist, followed the pattern of writing a complete manuscript for one of his weekly sermons and then preached his second sermon without notes. He wrote:

> By writing one sermon a week I hoped for precision, clarity, and terseness in expression; by preaching a sermon without writing every week, I hoped to develop the freeness and readiness of the true extempore style. Each method helped the other. The people never knew my methods, nor could they have distinguished any difference in the preparation of my preaching.[71]

Even though Sangster prepared by writing a complete manuscript he did not think a preacher should take it into the pulpit. He believed listeners valued a conversational style and that reading a manuscript hindered that freedom.

> It needs hardly to be said that, because a man writes a manuscript in his study, he is not compelled to read it from his pulpit desk. On the contrary, one greatly hopes that he will do no such thing.... Every preacher should be free of his manuscript, and not too tied to his notes. If you have got something from God to say to the people, it is better to look them in the face when you say it.[72]

Dietrich Bonhoeffer (1906-1945) stands in the middle of the twentieth century as a prophet-martyr. Executed in Nazi Germany just as the war was ending, his books have impacted several generations since. While he encouraged his students to write out their sermons completely, it seems that he did not use a manuscript in the pulpit. 'Rather he committed blocks of thought to memory and left the individual words to come as they would.'[73]

> The preacher should not begin to write his sermon until he has placed his thoughts in a clear outline. The outline will also help the preacher learn the sermon for delivery. He writes, 'A sermon that is difficult to learn is not a good one, or at least it is not a clear one.'
>   Bonhoeffer did not recommend memorization of the words of the sermon, but of the thoughts. He believed that the words would

take care of themselves if the general thought-blocks were remembered. Nor did he recommend taking a sheet of brief notes into the pulpit. He regarded the practice as having doubtful value. Nevertheless, even after the sermon has been written and committed to memory, it is not yet a sermon. He quoted Bezzel as saying that the sermon must be born twice, in the study and in the pulpit. 'Everything that has happened in the pastor's study is only preparation for the genuine birth of the sermon in the pulpit.' Once in the pulpit, the preacher should not rely on rhetorical tricks but understand that his preparation frees him to allow the Word to proceed naturally.[74]

Gerald Kennedy served as president of the Methodist Council of Bishops in America while at the same time preached regularly at the First United Methodist Church of Pasadena, California, in the mid-twentieth century.

Kennedy begins his weekly sermon preparation on Wednesday morning, 'and it takes an event of almost catastrophic significance to swerve me from my beginning at this particular time'. He first develops an outline from his text and scribbles down notes 'which I will have difficulty in deciphering'.

These notes suggest the development of the main points of the sermon. Then Kennedy lays aside his material until the next day; 'The next morning I take the outline and scratchy notes into a room where I can talk it out loud. This seems to me important because preaching is not only bringing thoughts to people, it is also finding words to make the thoughts march.'

Kennedy is a firm believer in oral preparation. After his initial practice delivery of the sermon, he speaks it again to himself again on Friday morning and again Saturday morning, and then parts of it again early Sunday morning: 'By that time I am ready to preach without any notes.' By following this oral method of preparation Kennedy spends less than four hours in the preparation of his sermons. This small amount of time is deceptive, since Kennedy begins long-range planning of his sermons a year in advance and devotes hours of daily study to the Bible, readings in theology, literature, and current events. Because of his constant oral preparation, Kennedy has developed an excellent conversational style.... Kennedy insists upon using a clear outline: 'While some novels can be invertebrates ... sermons cannot.' He likens a sermon without a clear outline to a telephone directory – a great cast but no plot. 'There is often an excuse for a poor sermon but there is never an excuse for a poor outline, or worse yet, for none at all.'[75]

One of the most mesmerizing preachers of the twentieth century was Martin Luther King, Jr. (1929-1968). His sermon, 'I Have a Dream', may be the most memorable of our time.

> During the first years of his ministry he spent at least fifteen hours on each sermon. He outlined the sermon on Tuesday, gathered material on Wednesday, and wrote his manuscript on Friday and Saturday. As his pace became more hectic he did not have time for such deliberate preparation, so he worked from a brief outline. He frequently reworked and reused earlier sermons. Often he spoke extemporaneously.[76]

While an overview of orality in preaching presents a compelling case for its advantages, the power of personal history usually provides the greatest incentives possible. In his book *You Are The Message,* Roger Ailes, a leading communications consultant, suggests a humble experience in self-examination regarding communication effectiveness:

> Take a piece of paper and list three times in your life when you know you've communicated successfully. Think about those times. What made them work? I'm sure of a few things: You were committed to what you were saying, you knew what you were talking about, and you were so wrapped up in the moment you lost *all* feelings of self-consciousness.[77]

Those three factors come close to a working description of orality. I know that my list of three quickly proved orality to win out in my preaching history.

CHAPTER 5

THE CRAFT OF ORALITY

For those who have either observed great oral preachers or who have from time to time experienced the power of orality during their own preaching, it is not difficult to appreciate the fruitfulness and fulfillment of preaching in an oral style. Ultimately orality comes to the issue of preaching without notes or with very few notes. That raises the issue of memory in preaching, which for even the most seasoned preacher unaccustomed to note-free preaching can be an issue of courage. R. W. Dale, the great Birmingham preacher admitted in his Yale lectures in 1905:

> It seems to me that the overwhelming weight of the argument is on the side of extemporaneous preaching; but I have very rarely the courage to go into the pulpit without carrying with me the notes of my sermon, and occasionally I read every sentence from the first to the last.[1]

Since we may hope that the greatest investment of courage in preaching should not need to be in sermonic delivery, we need to consider the practical issue of approach and preparation for preaching orally. During my own years of ministry training and practice, I have noticed how many give honor to orality in preaching or speak highly of preaching without notes but who provide little help and guidance in how to go about doing it. The focus of this chapter is on the practical progression from preparation to delivery in oral preaching.

Memory

The role of memory in preaching comes down to a very practical reality: if the preacher cannot remember what it is he wants to

say after hours of thoughtful preparation, why should there be
any hope that a congregation will remember much of the sermon
after having heard it just once? If fear of forgetting so
overwhelms the preacher, it is only logical that the same danger
of forgetting will even more powerfully afflict the congregation,
except they will be spared the public embarrassment. It seems
a fair rule of thumb that what a preacher can remember of the
sermon *just before* preaching it is far more than what the
congregation can remember *anytime after* they have heard it. If
it is important that a sermon be remembered, then we must ask
why memory has a rather low place of importance in the work
of many preachers. That low place is revealed by their use of
notes. Memory may be thought of as the 'eye of the needle' in
preaching. Everything that the preacher cannot remember to
say becomes excluded and does not reach the congregation.
Everything that the congregation cannot remember becomes
extraneous and does not enter into the life of the hearer beyond
the moment of delivery. Whatever else may be said about
preaching with notes, the practice does insulate the preacher
from having to confront the unrelenting reality that memory is
the foundational way in which sermons live beyond the moment.
A preacher who is willing to come to terms with memory will
be a more effective servant of the word of God.

It is important to remember that there are two aspects to true
craft: the deeply personal and spiritual roots that motivate the
work and the technical wisdom that gives expression to the work.
Nowhere is this more true than in orality in preaching.
Obviously, there must be an ability to remember the essential
elements of the sermon if it is to be preached without depending
on written notes. The issue of memory in speaking finds its
roots in the ancient oral cultures and had its greatest flowering
in Greek rhetoric before it was interwoven with medieval
mysticism. Enormous emphasis was placed on memory, not
only in pre-literate oral cultures, but also in the flowering of
Greek thought and in the pre-Enlightenment era.[2] Walter Ong
summarizes this vast amount of thought:

The principle basis for all the memory arts, Miss Yates finds, is the imaginative organization of space and spatially arranged imagery. One visualizes some kind of structure in space made up of recognizable parts standing in fixed relations to one another and then associates what one wishes to memorize with the various parts of the structure.[3]

The importance of organization and association are keys to memory and as we progress in developing an understanding of memory, we will discover how little literacy equips us to remember what we prepare to say in the sermon. Ong further summarizes the work of people such as Eric Havelock[4] when he notes:

This work on oral memory would seem to suggest some reason why Cicero, Martianus Capella, and other memory artists minimize 'memory for words' in favor of 'memory for things' – their oral mnemonic cultural background was thematic and formulaic rather than verbatim and in part a relic of mankind's original oral, prechirographic culture.[5]

The focus on remembering 'things' such as ideas or experiences rather than specific words is a major piece of any memory methodology. The ability of the mind to retain experience and connected experiences is far greater than the ability to retain words themselves, since words are symbolic reductions and distillations of actual experience and therefore more elusive to the human mind and personality.

Closely related to this preference for 'things' over 'words' is the Hebrew-Christian religious tradition:

This religious tradition differs from all others in being the religion of historical memory, an event-religion, built on remembrance of what God did for His Chosen People and culminating for Christians when the great memory feast of the Passover is transformed and focused for all time in the Last Supper, where Jesus says, 'Do this in memory of me.' This fact provides positive historical background for much of the Christian attention to memory as well as for the suspicion under which most memory 'arts' have ultimately tended to fall among Christians.[6]

We can describe this tradition as emphasis on concrete experience over abstract thinking. The New Testament makes much of the word 'witness' in telling the Christian story. Witnesses tell what they have seen and experienced more than trying to remember complex and extended ideas that they must recite from memory. Orality and memory make a far less threatening obstacle for the preacher than the attempt to create a literary based sermon which the preacher then struggles to memorize. If preaching without notes is to be delivered from being impossibly *difficult* there must be an approach that is significantly *different*.

In his foundational book, *Expository Preaching without Notes*, Charles Koller suggests that pulpit preparation might be divided into 50% for saturation, 40% for organization, and 10% for memorization. I suggest these three components might be considered as the quest for oral clarity.

Clarity

The concept of oral clarity must stand at the base of oral preaching because unless oral categories are introduced early into the preparation, either a major shift later in preparation will result in the loss of significant time or the possibility of remembering the sermon for oral delivery will be beyond reach. Oral clarity begins with recognizing that beneath the literary framework of much of the Bible is a strong undercurrent of orality. The great Old Testament narratives, the stories and teachings of the Gospels and even the dictated letters of the New Testament all bear the marks of having been born in the mouth before being delivered by the pen. Robert Ensign observes:

> Any liturgist/preacher who is aware of the dynamics of oral expression will immediately encounter a problem: virtually all

commentaries on biblical texts interpret them as written forms. This approach, as we have seen, limits the nature of interpretation and may ultimately work against what the liturgist/preacher hopes to accomplish: to interpret texts as expressed orally in a liturgical setting. Further, though commentaries at times trace the oral history of a text, they assume that a text will function the same whether written or expressed.[7]

In the early stages of preparation the preacher needs to be aware that while commentaries are useful for dealing with the historical context and grammar of the text, they may contain a subtle current that can quietly move him away from the ultimate goal, to declare God's word orally through this text. While much of the biblical text gives itself to following the flow of the argument, it may well be not only beyond but beside the point to seek a detailed outline of the passage. While written language can be reduced to grammatical diagramming, the result may be a truncated and reduced version of the thought that first came from the author. The point is not to destroy the integrity of the text, but rather to look carefully for signs of oral flow in it that will come closer to the preacher's ultimate task in speaking the sermon. While some advocate referring to commentaries later in the preparation process, I would argue for using commentaries quite early. At this stage the purpose is to deal with the literary concerns in the text and to become settled on its essential meaning and direction. The later commentaries are used in the process, the more likely it is that the sermon will be cast in more literary than oral forms. In whatever time is given for preparation, care should be taken that commentaries do not intrude into the time needed for creating the sermon itself. William Sangster made the arresting comment that should drive every honest preacher to self-examination: 'Ministers probably waste more time over reading than over anything else. Thinking and praying are our great needs.'[8] The plea, of course, is not for ignorant outpouring of passion, but rather for a thoughtful involvement with the Scripture after having done careful and disciplined work in the commentaries. Congregations instinctively are not seeking to know what the preacher has read but rather what the preacher has wrestled with and discovered from the Scripture to be God's message for this hour.

In a book devoted to the subject of preaching without notes, Hugh Litchfield draws together the elements of oral clarity under the concepts of simplifying the sermon, picturing the sermon, imagining the sermon and absorbing the sermon.[9] For the purposes of orality, simplifying the sermon must begin early in the preacher's interaction with the text and commentaries. Using imagery closely related to Greek and medieval frameworks for memory, Litchfield likens the sermon to finding the right road map. He describes the components of homiletical development as the Basic Route which is the Central Idea of the text and should be stated in a simple statement in the context of the text (for example: 'With God's help, David killed Goliath'). The Interstate is the Thesis of the sermon, which should be the single idea to be preached in terms of what the sermon text means now (for example: 'With God's help, we can kill our giants'). The Destination is the General Objective or the Purpose of the Sermon. Litchfield has developed six general areas from which to identify the purpose: Evangelistic, Supportive, Doctrinal/ Teaching, Devotional, Ethical, Consecrational.[10] This general destination will be further refined from the large area of intention to The House or the Specific Objective. The Specific Objective identifies the goal of persuasion to an identifiable action (for example, 'That they will, with God's help, kill their giants'). Litchfield calls the Specific Objective the 'thesis with legs'.[11] He calls the Trip Name, The Title. Sermon Development he calls Signposts, the several 'mini-destinations along the way'. This deals with the homiletical issues of points, steps, moves or divisions drawn from the text.[12] He completes this homiletical journey by describing The Final Map: The Cover Page, which contains these elements:

Text:
Title:
Central Idea of the Text: (Biblical truth, past tense)
Thesis: (Present tense, contemporary, personal)
General Objective: (Evangelistic, Supportive, Doctrinal/
Teaching, Devotional, Ethical, Consecrational)
Specific Objective:
Body: The Significant Signposts of the sermon development.

Developing – and learning – such a cover page is an essential step in learning how to preach without notes. It focuses our sermon and serves as the overarching framework for it. This cover page information is like the final road map that we determine will help us take our journey. It is the basic road plan. The cover page is the basic road map for our sermon journey. If we memorize anything (and I do not stress outright memorization in my system), let us memorize the cover page. Honestly, I do not think remembering it will be too much of a problem. As hard as we have worked to get our idea and objective and sermon signposts, how can we forget them? The week before we preach, those items get 'into our blood stream' and become a part of us. We cannot forget them! When this happens, we are on our way to preaching without notes.[13]

While much of Litchfield's method is common to homiletical preparation, the holistic approach that his 'cover page' employs does create a shift to a more oral framework that makes memory more achievable. An important addition to Litchfield's system needs to be considered. The Thesis and the Signposts need to be expressed in strongly oral terms. The widely held importance of the Main Idea often seems to fall short of being a statement that is orally memorable. Main Ideas that are primarily literary in their expressions will fall into the danger of being hard to remember and perhaps even unfriendly to the tongue. The Main Idea or Thesis needs to take on the oral quality of an aphorism.

The preacher would do well to study the Proverbs, not just to find wisdom, but to see that many of the aphoristic statements of that book provide practical help in framing memorable thoughts. Such thoughts will reflect the qualities of a Main Idea that can be stated, repeated, restated with slightly different words and brought back again at the end to solidify this idea in the mind and memory of the hearer. The oral quality of the Main Idea is a key to clarity. Closely related to the orality of the Main Idea is the oral power of Litchfield's 'Signposts'. While common practice has encouraged the use of complete sentences for the points or moves of the sermon, I suggest that those sentences must be terse and formed with a series of words in an oral pattern (alliteration, assonance or some other kind of oral parallelism). Long sentences without oral quality will tend to bring an overload of words that will tax the preacher's memory and will probably not translate into memorable Signposts for the hearer. R. E. O. White speaks to my own experience when he affirms, 'The secret of such freedom and power lies in memorizing *ideas* and not *words*.... The sermon which *depends* upon keeping to one's notes probably owes too much to form and phrasing. Its content is too thin to stand up in everyday clothes.'[14]

This approach may also be thought of as paragraphic thinking rather than sentence-by-sentence. Oliver and Cortright develop this thinking:

Successful *extemporaneous* speaking is the result of careful preparation and even memorization of facts and ideas, but not the precise words to be used. This preparation is *idea-centered*, not *word-centered*. When you give this kind of speech, you have the maximum opportunity to 'reproduce' the line of thinking you have carefully prepared while you 'create' the verbal/gestural pattern in which it is given. Your preparation consists in mastering your facts until you may *know* various styles of modern music, or the characteristics of your favorite movie stars or athletes. Your preparation also involves organizing your facts into a pattern that suits your purpose. This pattern, like your facts, you will *know*, for it has resulted from your careful consideration of how best to arrange the sequence and relationship of your facts. Trying to remember only words makes you little more than a machine, a phonograph. Then when you forget some of the words, your mind goes blank. You have been remembering instead of thinking, but if you have your facts and your organization solidly mastered and are formulating your actual words and sentences out of the speaking situation, you have achieved the ideal combination of reproduction and creativity.[15]

While the danger of not expressing a finished idea in a complete sentence may exist, the equal danger is that a full sentence crafted on paper may not penetrate the preacher's memory sufficiently to serve the oral function. In a recent sermon I found the three words: 'Destiny, Distance, and Duty' sufficient pegs upon which I could rest a sermon on the parable of the Good Samaritan. While none of these words bore the weight of the full thought in each of these moves, I had no difficulty in recalling what was involved in each of these parts of the sermon.

Richard Storrs spoke of the practical difficulty of excessive written materials that brought him early frustration in preaching without notes:

I saw at a glance what the secret of the failure had been. I had made too much preparation in detail; had written out heads, subdivisions, even some passages or paragraphs in full, in order that I might be certain beforehand to have material enough at command and the result of it was that I was all the time looking backward, not forward, in preaching; trying to remember, not only prearranged trains of thought but particular forms of expression, instead of trusting to the impulse of the subject, and seeking to impress certain great and principle features of it on the congregation.

My verbal memory has always been the weakest part of my mental organization. I hardly dare trust myself now to quote a sentence from any writer, without having it before me in manuscript. I had wholly overloaded this verbal memory, in my preparation for the service; and the inevitable consequence was that it and I staggered along together.[16]

Oral craft will soon bring the preacher to face the question of what to do with extended quotations that must be accurately stated. Over the months of my own practice (and following the counsel of others such as Macartney), I have found that the necessity of exact quotations is far less important than I once thought.[17] If poetry is to be used, it should not be 'heavy' poetry that requires close interpretation. Much great poetry simply goes by the ear too quickly to be taken in. Familiar hymns need to be memorized and quoted freely so that their emotive power is truly experienced. On occasion there may be a story or a written piece that does something very important for the sermon. On those rare moments, it is best to make the most of reading and pull a paper from a pocket and make no apology for reading it. If reading has become a very rare act, the change will create its own attention for the congregation.

An important part of ensuring the clarity of thought in the Signposts and in moving from one to another is the attention to transitions. In my own experience I have had little concern for the importance of transitions while I was preaching in a literary framework. I was concerned that the main points were clearly stated in complete sentences but the relation of one to the next didn't strike me as very important. Only when I began to use one word to capture the larger idea of the sermonic part did I find myself rather naturally giving attention to how I would get from one point to the next. It began to be clear that transitions are more important in oral communication than they are in sermons cast in a literary frame. Paul Borden places transitions at the core of being able to preach without notes. In a class lecture he taught that the primary outline points should be interconnected, not just connected to the big idea. It is important to write out the connection between I and II and between II and III. If a preacher cannot write them into the outline, he doesn't know them. When a preacher can clearly express the transitions, a large step has been taken to noteless preaching. In preaching from memory, if the preacher forgets the next point, the problem is probably a weak or illogical connection. Following the flow of the thought from one point to the next with the help of carefully considered connections is a key to memory.[18] I have discovered that transitions become key moments of sensitivity to the congregation's involvement with me. Have I said enough? Have I raised a problem or an obstacle that I should address before moving on? If I am ready to move on, how do I best bring the congregation with me as I introduce the next Signpost along the way? On occasion I find that my prepared transition needs adjustment or replacement in the present chemistry of the preaching moment. When I am sensitive to this, I can sense the involvement of the congregation with me. David James Burrell quotes Professor Pattison:

> The management of his transitions marks the practiced preacher. They are the bridges of discourse, and by them he passes from one to the other, while for lack of them the preacher finds himself trembling on the edge of some great gulf with no means to get across to his next thought.[19]

While all that has been said here about 'simplifying' may seem far from simple, the process that keeps moving to intentional clarity will take on the feel of simplicity. William Sangster has expressed it well:

> There can be no clear speaking without clear thinking. No man can hope to be lucid in the pulpit (or anywhere else for that matter) who has not first *thought* himself clear. Nothing can take the place of disciplined thought. Only those who have gone over and over their theme in their minds and seen the path they intend to take from the announcement of the text to the concluding sentence can have any confidence in the clarity they will achieve. No man need (or ought!) to burden his mind with memorized words. If the thought is clear, adequate words can be commanded in the moment of utterance (and the ability to do this greatly increases with practice), but the thought *must* be clear and the path plainly in view.[20]

Imagery

Another aspect of oral clarity that is essential to memory is translating clear thought into mental pictures and images. Again, it is important to remember that memorable preaching has a dual importance: every preacher hopes that his congregation will remember the sermon but even more important, every preacher who preaches without notes *must* remember the sermon. The often cited experience of remembering sermon illustrations while forgetting the point simply affirms that pictures and imagery create the most memorable communication for both speaker and hearer.

It is important for the preacher to come to terms with the issues of imagery in preaching, because it is at the point of imagery that orality may encounter a serious conflict with values of literacy. While this collision of values may not be contemplated in these terms and may not even be a conscious conflict, the careful student of the text of Scripture may face an unidentified tension that needs to be addressed. Bryan Chapell recounts a conversation with an academic who was complaining about the prominence of illustrations in contemporary preaching. Chapell relates the conversation:

> 'All we do is entertain people,' he said. 'It is not enough just to preach. Now we must tell stories and be comedians. It's all because of TV. People just cannot sit and think anymore. We have to parade illustrations before them like hosts of a variety show. I will sprinkle some illustrations in my sermons because I must in order to make people listen, but how I hate it.'[21]

I suspect that more than anything else, this sense of the unworthiness of story with its innate relationship to picture and image rests in the tension between orality and literacy. Of course, imagery and story can be abused in preaching, but it is also true that more troublesome problems have occurred in preaching that lacks picture and imagery in its language. This stark prose forces the listener to struggle, become weary and finally give up on the sermon because the language is more fitted for the eye than for the ear. The eye has a far greater capacity to pause, reflect, go back and digest the words on a page than a listener with even a very keen mind and a strongly focused attention can command. Preaching, with its personal and relational power, simply must have a greater use of imagery for both the preacher and the listener to grasp the content. Preachers who write and writers who preach need to be deeply aware of those differences. Even in the most dense theological discourses of Paul's letters, he was writing to church congregations and was using language that he fully expected them to understand and absorb. In fact, his most theological writing is filled with words that are picture-based semantic symbols. The context and meaning of words such as justification and propitiation suggest far more than arid definition. They cry out for careful and imaginative description and development that will fill the minds of both the preacher and the congregation with memorable pictures that adorn the walls of the imagination. This is not moving away from the text of the Bible, it is moving more deeply into it.

Warren Wiersbe quotes from the writing of Alfred North Whitehead concerning university education and applies it to the ministry of the Word:

> The university imparts information, but it imparts it imaginatively. At least, this is the function which it should perform for society. A university which fails in this respect has no reason for existence. This atmosphere of excitement, arising from imaginative consideration, transforms knowledge. A fact is no longer a bare fact: it is invested with all its possibilities. It is no longer a burden on the memory: it is energizing as the poet of our dreams, and as the architect of our purposes.... The tragedy of the world is that those who are imaginative have but slight experience, and those who are experienced have feeble imaginations. Fools act on imagination without knowledge; pedants act on knowledge without imagination. The task of university is to weld together imagination and experience.[22]

Wiersbe draws significant implications for the preacher to consider in terms of the role of imagination for the congregation's benefit. The essential point here, however, is that fact must be joined to imagination before it stops burdening the mind. Who has not struggled to remember dates for a history exam or vocabulary for a language requirement? When bare fact is clothed in a fuller relationship to the inner life, it no longer is hard to remember but now is impossible to forget. I find this to be at the very core of the preaching task and have begun to discover that literary values which are uncritically carried over to preaching will create a ballast on memory that makes orality impossible. Only when the careful exegetical studies have produced literary clarity, does the further work of the preacher begin. That clear word from Scripture must be taken and clothed with the meditation that brings life to raw linguistic fact. With great care Wiersbe emphasizes that imagination that creates metaphor is not the subject of the sermon. 'If handled properly, the metaphor expands the subject, illumines it and helps make it vivid and personal to our listeners; but the metaphor is not the message. Metaphor must never replace precise definition of doctrine.'[23]

The potential for abusing the magnetic power of imagination in using metaphor and story is always with the preacher but the imagination as a reflective response to the text and the theological integrity of Scripture is one of the preacher's most powerful sources in making orality and memory possible. Only when the preacher has gone beyond merely reading and understanding the text and has begun to deal with the impact and application of these words is the sermon being born. As long as there remains a point in the sermon where the preacher cannot freely talk about the issue at hand, the sermon is not ready to be preached. Again, Wiersbe speaks to the issue when he writes, 'Exegesis *empties* language and enriches us with facts; but imagination *fills* language and yields nourishing truths.'[24] Donald Sunukjian reflects this broader function of preaching when he says, 'The sermon is an "extended metaphor", which results in an understanding not only of *what* is said, but also *why* it is good wisdom and *where* it is operating or can operate in our lives.'[25] When the preacher has richly furnished the galleries of the mind with vividly drawn pictures from the biblical text, not only has the Bible come alive to him but now the very fullness and passion that the congregation hungers to hear has been born. It is a technical side benefit that this living picture creates a soaring memory that frees the preacher from notes and allows the listener to carry the sermon deeply embedded in the folds of the heart, mind and will. Jay Adams, in an analysis of Spurgeon's preaching, writes:

> Spurgeon had only words with which to work. The extreme difficulty of word craftsmanship may be further discerned from the fact that these words had to be so fashioned that they would quicken the imagination by way of the memory. Memory contains the experience of various sense perceptions stored away. But it possesses nothing not previously experienced. Spurgeon, therefore, had to know what experiences were common to his hearers. Then he had to frame his appeal with clarity, simplicity and interest (a difficult combination indeed) not only to awaken the memory but also to arouse vital interest. Ivory tower sermons do not do this. He had to live and move among his people and think about the best ways to reach them with the Word.[26]

The combination of benefits which Adams recounts serves further to underscore the fact that orality has a wealth of its own inter-connected dynamics which come together to create the power of oral preaching. Preachers who try merely to preach without notes but take no account of the issues of experience and imagination will create chaos both for themselves and for their listeners. It is not too much to say that if we do not value imagery and story and are instead committed to closely woven logic and abstraction there is little chance of preaching orally.

A significant question arises in treating closely woven theological passages in the New Testament letters. How does imagery relate to tightly constructed linear thought? While imagery may not be able to do justice to the particularity of a theological progression, the congregation may find little to hold on to without image and story being used to open windows of light along the way. When preaching theologically robust passages imagery and story are essential for creating a large vision and theme of the passage. This may require either dividing such a passage into shorter parts for the sermon text or selectivity in what is developed in such a text. I believe it is hazardous, however, to see such passages as standing outside the realm of imagery and story. Moreover preachers who delve richly into the world of experience and imagination to give full development to the message of a tightly constructed theological passage may find that detailed notes constrict the outflow of oral freedom and are unnecessary.

Structural clarity
An additional aspect of oral clarity for the preacher is structural clarity. Along with being clear in his thinking about the text's message and being rich in the mental imagery that fastens the message to pictures in the mind, the preacher needs to have the structural skeleton clearly in mind, particularly in the introduction and conclusion. Structural clarity is particularly important for the introduction because vagueness, drift and lack of flow must be overcome decisively from the first word. Opening words, whether they be a general recognition of the situation or the developing of a controlling metaphor contained in a story, must be clear to the preacher, not only for effective presentation but also for the innate sense of having a stepping off point. From the introductory words comes the raising of the issue to be dealt with and a strong move to relate that issue to the hearers' present concern. At this point the text may be introduced as speaking to this situation. These elements need to be kept in mind for the structure as well as for the content, for structure and content can very nicely complement each other as dual supports in remembering the introduction. Keeping

structure in mind also serves to provide maximum freedom should the immediate situation change requiring the preacher to adjust some part of the content to better respond to the situation. The longer the preacher has experience in consciously moving through these structures, the more at ease he will be no matter what the variations of content may be. Chapell suggests the following structural elements for the introduction:

> Arouse interest, introduce the subject (prepare for the proposition's concepts and terms), make it personal (identify the reason for the sermon), state the 'fallen condition focus' that causes us all to need this message, drive the need to the personal level, bond the sermon to the Scripture and attach the proposition.[27]

The body of the sermon needs structural support not only for clarity and flow but because it is the longest part of the sermon and requires several supports for memory. Paul Scott Wilson provides a helpful structural concept in dividing sermonic thought between metonymy (which creates order) and metaphor (which creates imagery).[28] Oral communication deeply depends on both. Order gives the listener the sense that the sermon is going somewhere, that it has movement and direction. Imagery provides the mental pictures that furnish the listener's mind with the 'living furniture' that gives life and longevity to the spoken word. These distinctions can be seen as significant structural memory supports. The vertical line indicates the metonymical flow that moves from one key thought to the next. That line can be joined with horizontal lines that indicate metaphorical key images and pictures (illustrations) attached to it. This creates a simple diagram (found on the next page) which the preacher can remember for each sermon as a structural road map:

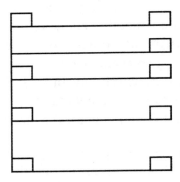

Without even representing the content of the main ideas or the supporting metaphorical material, this structural diagram of the sermon can rest in the memory and reinforces the preacher's sense of location. The previously discussed issue of a closely woven logical passage with imagery added for imaginative power is served well by this framework. The linear flow of the passage is clearly represented as is the supporting metaphorical material. The equally important benefit of giving the sermon structural clarity in its conception is an added value. The structural intentionality that balances metonymy and metaphor serves to protect the sermon from drift, one of the greatest dangers of oral preaching. This paradigm reflects some of the most ancient characteristics of the art of memory. From earliest times, the concept of memory as moving through the halls and rooms of a building stood at the base of memory. Each room and hallway was to be visualized as having part of the speech's content. The speaker literally was trained to move through the building of memory as the speech was uttered.[29]

The conclusion has its own issues of oral structure that need to be considered. Chapell summarizes the conclusion with a three part structure: *recapitulation, exhortation (motivation) and elevation (climax).* While these structural elements may vary, the importance of having clear elements both in preparation and in delivery are essential. Identifying these elements will undergird the memory as well as give strong intentional movement through some of the most vulnerable parts of the sermon. Clearly, the final exhortation and elevation must be carefully thought through in preparation, for the hope of allowing the moment to provide the climax is presumptuous at best. If, in fact, the preacher does have a spontaneous insight for the climax, it may well have come because the prepared climax gave freedom for the mind to search freely during the sermon for an ending that even more powerfully serves the moment.

Saturation

The last major consideration in the quest for oral clarity is what some homileticians call saturation (others call it absorption). How does the preacher take all the labor of preparation and gather it into a final form for preaching? How does the preparatory work of writing lead to the oral act of preaching? Should an oral presentation first be written out completely and then reduced to a memorable form, or should the orality rule the process and writing be kept to the minimum throughout? Some of the most carefully considered and fully developed thoughts on this critical point come from Clyde Fant in his book, *Preaching for Today*. Fant strongly urges a deep and early cleavage between written and oral communication. In tracing the emergence of the written sermon manuscript from the early church's oral culture, Fant argues that the sermon in the textual form which has developed in recent centuries is quite different from its earlier oral form.[30] From this history he concludes:

> What suits the ear does not suit the eye. What about the corollary of that law? Has it ever occurred to us that if spoken speech looks bad when transcribed, the opposite might also be true – *that written speeches sound bad when heard?* There are really no exceptions to this law although we've all heard sermons from manuscripts that seem to be. But in those cases, the manuscript has been forced to make radical concessions to the spoken medium.[31]

While few would disagree with this, it seems that there is great hope on the part of many homiletical theorists that the pen can be tamed to serve the purposes of orality. In response, Fant asserts:

> To overcome these difficulties, teachers of preaching have long advocated 'writing as you speak'. But that is a hybrid art that nobody teaches. Learning to speak and learning to write are difficult enough in themselves without learning to hybridize the two. And why do it anyway? Why not prepare for the oral medium in the first place?
>
> Preachers should realize that their problems don't stop once they have written a manuscript; in fact, they have just begun – now they *really* have a problem. What do they *do* with the manuscript? They have three alternatives – all bad. First, they can read the manuscript; nobody recommends that, for obvious reasons. Second, they can memorize it; nobody recommends that either. And third, they can get as familiar as possible with it in the study and then try to do without it as much as possible in the pulpit. This third alternative is the method generally recommended, but it still leaves preachers with plenty of problems.
>
> When preachers try to follow a manuscript mentally in the pulpit without having it with them, they present a curious sight. When they are successful in recalling the sermon, they sound polished and look poised – sometimes too polished and too poised, like a child delivering a piece learned for school. On the other hand, when they are unsuccessful, their word choice and syntax are radically different. They may also get a vacant look on their faces as they rummage around their mental attics trying to remember all those beautiful phrases they wrote and rewrote in the study.
>
> As for those preachers who take their manuscripts into the pulpit and try not to look at it, they usually look like preachers trying not to look at a manuscript. They may struggle valiantly to look the audience in the eye, but it is apparent that their hearts are not in it, and they keep sneaking furtive glances at the pages beneath their fingers. If they are bold enough to go ahead and look anyway, they often give the impression of a kiwi bird going to water; now the head is up, now the head is down. Meanwhile

the audience sits respectfully listening, as though hearing a sermon required great politeness – which in this case, it does. Active mental dialogue and personal encounter give way to polite listening. I know that some preachers can master the use of a manuscript so that their delivery is smooth and natural. Many of the finest preachers in Christian history preached exclusively from manuscripts. I know that. But that doesn't eliminate the problems I have described. They are still there, and the manuscript preachers who excel do so in spite of their manuscripts, not because of them.[32]

Because this matter of relating thoroughness to a full written preparation is so prevalent, before turning to specific methods of oral preparation, let Fant speak to the prejudice against preaching with less than a complete manuscript:

> For years preachers have been intimidated by the 'ideal' of these great preachers and their polished manuscripts. They have been asked, 'Isn't preaching worth the effort? Can we afford to go into the pulpit half-prepared?' Karl Barth has even warned darkly that we will be held accountable for every idle word in the day of judgment and used this scripture (Matt. 12:36) as a proof-text for the absolute necessity of a manuscript. (We will not take this as a typical example of the great exegete.) Naturally he equates anything else with a lack of preparation.
>
> But are these really the alternatives? Is preparation versus unpreparation, the careful manuscript versus the offhanded talk? Is there no other approach that can prepare us as carefully and as thoroughly as the manuscript, or more so, and that connects us more directly with the true oral medium for the sermon?[33]

Before answering that question, it is helpful to reflect on Barth's strong condemnation of unwritten sermons.[34] Of all theologians who it would seem should have a deep respect for the existential utterance in the proclamation of God's Word, Barth should lead the list. However, in our academic and ecclesiastical tradition writing holds a great power over our consciences. I admit that I needed a clear and reasoned basis for moving from a strongly literary preparation to an orally based preparation.

Fred Craddock reflects on this process of preparation as well. Toward the end of his book, *Preaching*, he writes:

> We have not talked yet of writing anything, and deliberately so. It would be a mistake to think that the goal of all this work is to write a sermon; it is not. The goal is to preach, and writing is a servant, nothing more, nothing less, of that goal. Let a preacher begin thinking that the point is to get a Sunday's sermon written, and a string of negative results follow. In the first place, the written sermon is a kind of closure which offers not only a sense of satisfaction – thank God, I'm finished with it! – but also a shutting down of germination and gestation, often prematurely. Being finished, being able to walk away and attend to other things, is so attractive a prospect that it can inch forward into the thinking, feeling and imagining, forming process and put periods where commas, dashes, and question marks are still at work.
>
> Second, to make writing the sermon the goal of the process is to cause one to think writing, rather than speaking, throughout the preparation. Preaching is oral communication and to do it most effectively the minister needs to image himself or herself, talking with the parishioners as the sermon is being formed. The vast difference between orality and textuality will become apparent as the minister prepares as speaker not as writer. In textuality, there is more often an overload of information while orality tends to adjust quantity to the brevity and fragility of the communicative moment. Oral presentations cluster ideas and images by association; written presentations arrange ideas and illustrative materials in a linear sequence like words on a page. Writing tends to be more abstract.
>
> A third negative result of making the writing of the sermon one's preparatory goal is that this approach creates for the preacher the very difficult task of getting the message off the page again and into the air. Preparation that moves *toward* writing must soon thereafter make a radically different move: *from* writing to speaking.... Some preachers who write the sermon and then lay it aside until Saturday night or Sunday morning never seem to return to it with comfort. They handle the manuscript in the pulpit as

though it belonged to someone else. The very use of a manuscript is spoken of as one would speak of a weakness or of a rule broken, with the tones of confession. Some give the impression of uncertainty, as when some important decision has long been postponed. Shall I memorize it? Shall I read it but make every effort to disguise the reading? Or shall I come clean and simply read it without pretending otherwise?.... Much of the awkwardness and discontinuity created by writing and then oralizing a text can be relieved by preparing orally from the outset.[35]

Clyde Fant has given direction for the development of an oral sermon that is as helpful as any I have come upon.[36] He is careful to emphasize that oral preaching is not to be the product of disastrous nonpreparation:

If the preacher had to choose between doing without careful sermon preparation and doing without direct contact with the audience, I suppose he or she should do without direct contact with the audience. But that's like deciding which eye to see with. You don't have to make that choice.[37]

Fant then develops a basic methodology that moves through all the stages of preparation:

1. Initial Study

'The oral preparation method begins exactly like the manuscript method.'[38] This is an important statement that covers a great deal of what has been omitted in this project. Oral preaching is *not* a shortcut or a diminishing of the disciplines of exegesis. Orality in no way seeks to treat the text lightly or merely as a springboard into personal conversation between a preacher and the congregation with the Bible being little more than a means of getting started. *All* the concerns of the text must be cared for. The focus of this stage of preparation concerns the theme of the sermon and the basic directional sentences or steps in the development of this theme. Fant regards this stage as both exegetical and meditative. His contribution to the uniqueness of orality begins with the statement:

To this point, the preparation of the sermon is a matter of thought, but beyond this early stage it should be a matter of speech. The tentative direction of the sermon that thought has suggested should be made definite through speaking. We begin with the rough oral draft.[39]

This point has been a major issue of thought and change for me, for over the years I have tended to spend far more time in exegetical work and in the thought level of the text than with the equally important issue of how the message of the text should be spoken. Often I have found myself confronting the moment to preach having spent a disproportionate amount of time at the literary thought level with an inadequate amount of time given to how the message should be spoken. Grant Osborne touches on the tension when he writes on the demands of developing sermonic style:

Style is the instrument by which the sermon becomes memorable. The great preaching stylists (such as Edwards, Barnhouse, Swindoll) have all worked as hard on presentation as they have on exegesis. Unfortunately, in many circles style has replaced content. Many spend far more time on packaging than on determining the truth content. The reason is obvious: poor content with good style will satisfy many, while good content with poor style will satisfy few. Yet style must always remain a supplement to the message of the text rather than an end in itself.[40]

Joseph Stowell, in a printed interview with Haddon Robinson, reflects on moving beyond the exegetical phase of preparation:

I perceive sermon preparation in two phases. One the skill phase; the other is the creative phase. The skill phase focuses on the exegetical outline. That's the easiest part of sermon preparation. My weakest sermons have been ones I preached when I finished the skill phase and did not take time to let it germinate and, as John Stott says, 'Take it into the world of real people.' It's like fixing a meal. You can buy the groceries and set them on the counter and say, 'Okay, there it is.' It's quite another thing to get the recipe out and mix the groceries together and put the food on the table. You might even go a step further and make a great, attractive, nourishing feast. My goal is to prepare a meal that's both nourishing and attractive.... You've got to have time to be creative. I begin doing my exegesis no later than Monday. Some ministers do it three to four weeks ahead. As a busy pastor, I was never able to accomplish that. For me, the skill stage and the creative stage don't happen sequentially; they happen together. As I do my exegesis, I keep a pad of paper handy and write down creative ideas that come to me. I have to capture the creative thoughts before they leave me. Creative ideas come and I think I'll never forget them, but the next day they're gone.[41]

Perhaps each preacher has a unique struggle to keep some kind of appropriate proportion between the textual disciplines and the oral requirements of preaching. I know it is a decision I continually need to clarify and be intentional about.

2. The Rough Oral Draft

Fant conceives this phase as writing each of the tentative directional sentences or major movements of the theme on a separate sheet of paper. He recommends preaching out loud on each of these movements as long as ideas suggest themselves, keeping pen in hand and pausing in speaking only long enough to note briefly the key directional phrases or sentences that emerge.

Each of these sentences should introduce a *thought block* that has really struck the heart of the concern of the text or of the people. These phrases correspond with the topic sentence of the paragraphs in a manuscript. But in this case they do not introduce a paragraph – no one speaks in paragraphs – but a thought block, 'something I want to talk about', which may represent one or more minutes of oral development.

This stage corresponds exactly with the writing of the rough draft of the manuscript – *except that it is being done in the medium that will eventually be used.* The composition is oral, not written, and the difference can be plainly seen in the final product. Verbal fluency will jump dramatically using this method. And rather than practicing on your audience, you are practicing on yourself.[42]

The arrangement of all this is still fluid and subject to revision. The ideas are being clarified and refined as you go and the decisions of order and the introduction of imagery and illustration are yet to be made. Once a basic flow for the body of the sermon has been established, it is time to make decisions about the introduction and conclusion. This concludes the rough draft of the oral manuscript.

3. The Final Oral Manuscript

In the final stage decisions are made about including, excluding and arranging the main thought blocks and transitional material. Because you have heard your sermon, you have the ability to make necessary changes. Now preach it out loud again. Try to preach through the material without looking at it. If the development is simple and accurate it should not be hard. If there are places you cannot move through easily, it is likely that part of the sermon has a problem that needs to be addressed. The key issue here is that the work is being done in the medium in which the sermon will be preached – orality.

4. The Sermon Brief

The result of the oral process is a tool or instrument for the preacher to keep and refer to. It is not a sermon outline or a manuscript, but a *sermon brief*. Fant pictures this page or page and a half as looking something like the diagram on the next page.[43]

In the lines under the basic directional sentence are key sentences, each introducing its own thought block of discussion. (Exploring the biblical material and the contemporary situation; presenting pictorial, illustrative material, etc.)

Fant summarizes the advantages of this approach:

Sermon Brief

_____

_____

3-5 sentences   Introduction: _____

_____

_____

Basic Directional Sentence (Division)

_____

_____

_____

_____

Basic Directional Sentence (Division) (etc.)

_____

3-5 sentences   Conclusion:_____

_____

_____

---

1. The sermon has produced the instrument rather than the instrument producing the sermon.
2. It is truer to the nature of conversation because it is less rigid and more adaptable.
3. It does not tie the preacher to the wording of a manuscript. There is room for creativity and spontaneity in the preaching moment. Something *happens* between a preacher and congregation; everything has not already happened in the study. The manuscript gives the impression of an event rather than being the event itself. It offers the possibility of having a true dialogue with the congregation.
4. The sermon brief gives more focus and direction than a bare outline. The brief protects against the impression of unpreparedness, vagueness, or aimless wandering. It helps stay 'on track'.
5. The oral process of preparation results in an oral product for the oral medium of preaching.[44]

Fant further helps the preacher to preach without even the sermon brief by suggesting these preparatory questions:

1. What is the main concern of this sermon (purpose, theme, subject)?
2. What do I want to say about that (order, movement, main divisions)?
3. How do I begin (opening movement)?
4. How do I proceed within the first movement, the second, etc. (mental review of the order of basic directional sentences)?
5. How do I conclude (final thought block)?[45]

All these steps of preparation have been under the concern of absorption or saturation. The question of how to proceed from this stage brings a division of responses. Some, such as Litchfield, hold strongly that after the sermon brief has been constructed the sermon should then be written out to encourage additional clarity of thought and appropriateness of expression although Fant seems not to agree. Fant at least seems to imply that writing out a manuscript will likely bring dynamics of textuality into the preacher's mind and create an unhelpful memory burden. Litchfield, on the other hand, strongly urges that the discipline of writing will save the preacher from unformed and vague expression and commends it as an important part of the oral process. I find that writing particularly critical parts of the sermon are helpful so long as I pay attention to the oral quality needed to retain that portion and have it come alive in the preaching moment.

Litchfield then advocates several actual oral rehearsals of the sermon. It may be best at this issue to recognize that saturation and absorption may require somewhat different methods for different people and that varying circumstances may dictate that the same preacher adjust the preparation. Several issues do come to mind from personal experience, however. Unless there is a specific formulaic pattern to be worked out, or a simple and direct opening and closing statement, the danger of becoming literary still looms large over the preacher. When the importance of large portions of verbatim language becomes very extensive, anxiety over memory will likely burden the preacher.

There are two post-preaching disciplines that the oral preacher should consider. With the ease of recording sermons, the preacher should make a regular practice of listening to all that he preaches. This may be done while doing other things that do not require mental activity and will keep the preacher alert to verbal patterns or problems that need to be remedied. The tendency to drift, to linger longer on a point than is necessary, the over use of certain words, all come to the preacher's attention if time is spent each week with the recording of last Sunday's sermon. I find it helpful to go back occasionally to a sermon of some six months earlier to detect issues such as tendencies to abstraction, signs of fatigue, etc. A bit of distance from the event helps me to listen even to myself more objectively.

Alongside the recorded sermon is the discipline of writing. The discipline of writing still plays an important part in shaping and sharpening the preacher's verbal skills. The preacher makes a wise investment in preaching proficiency by doing other writing or even reducing last week's sermon to a written text. This will help develop sensitivity to style and grammar without imposing a textual dynamic on the actual preaching.

Koller has a helpful thought on the issue of saturation and the importance of allowing the sermon to pass through the preacher many times and in different ways:

> Whatever method of preparation the preacher may follow, he needs to be thoroughly familiar with his material. He must know the subject in all its ramifications. 'No man can be eloquent on a subject that he does not understand', as Cicero, the greatest orator of ancient Rome, declared two thousand years ago. Even inspiration cannot work in a vacuum.
>
> The preacher must not begrudge the time spent in gathering his factual data and preparing his Scripture analysis on the way to his sermon outline. 'It is a general principle that anything that costs the producer little is of little value to others.' One of the

penalties of plagiarism is that it so largely by-passes the processes of saturation. For the expenditure of time and thought and labor, there is no substitute. A good procedure is to select the sermon topic early; meditate upon it daily; let the sermon grow; then write the outline in one sitting.[46]

The great purpose of the oral craft is to create a sermon *inside* the preacher in all its fullness so that, when the moment to preach comes, the text of Scripture in all its meaning and significance pours forth from the preacher with purpose, clarity and order, passion and imagination, so that the hearers know that they have heard from a servant of the word of the Lord.

CHAPTER 6

WHAT DIFFERENCE IS ORALITY MAKING IN MY PREACHING?

Anthony Trollope is quoted as saying in *Barchester Towers*, 'There is, perhaps, no greater hardship at present inflicted on mankind in civilized and free countries, than the necessity of listening to sermons'.[1] While listening to sermons may be difficult, for the conscientious preacher who hungers to honor the word of God and serve his hearers, the creating of sermons also has its hardships. Through exploring the values and dynamics of orality I have experienced a new depth of spiritual realities which the Scriptures call forth from the preacher who gives himself to this form of preaching. While careful and patient exegetical work remains foundational, orality creates, at least for me, a new range of inner responses to God's truth that I must move through in order to preach with power. I have discovered a need for internalizing the message both imaginatively and logically. Without these inner disciplines I simply will not have the authenticity and ability to remember the clear message that orality requires. I have discovered that in my own experience a more fully written out manuscript may actually cover over less careful and thoughtful preparation. The activity and form of the writing process can imply for me a level of preparation that is less than complete.

I have also learned that I have needed to move into orality at my own pace. In his classic plea for orality Clarence Macartney argued for an all or nothing approach to preaching without notes: 'But if a man has set himself to preach without notes, he ought never – even under trying conditions – to fall away from it and go back to a manuscript. It is far better to fail now and then without a complete manuscript than to run the risk of being bound by one.'² For the more timid, and especially for those who do not see themselves as naturally possessing the inclinations to orality, a gradual approach that experiments and moves back and forth between orality and literacy is more likely to be beneficial. My own experience is similar to that of Craig Loscalzo who wrote: 'I moved from reading a full manuscript in the pulpit to preaching with extended note cards to preaching without notes.'³ For me this gradual move began with using many carefully placed post-it notes in my Bible to reducing these more and more while becoming increasingly free of the pulpit. I suspect that my being able to experience the value of each stage of progression and sensing the increased level of effectiveness at each stage has made the process of transition more natural and less distracting both for me and the congregation. At this point I have not completely abandoned my last small post-it note, but intend to continue working toward that goal.

I have also learned that orality comprises only part of the entire preaching task. It is by no means a universal cure for all the ills of preaching, or at least my preaching. There is an ever-present danger that oral freedom can encourage inadequate work in the text. Orality without careful thought and preparation can create loose and static communication. I am learning each week that introductions and conclusions must be more considered and crafted than before. I particularly am aware of the importance of a strong and well-prepared transition into the main body of the sermon. An oral introduction easily becomes too long and rambling without clear, concise wording and movement. On more than one Sunday I have lingered too long in the introduction because I was not propelled by sufficiently prepared words and process to arrive effectively at the first point.

Orality has created a greater consciousness of how important the gestation period is in creating a sermon. Perhaps the inner workings of preachers vary in this regard, but I find that the more time between first conceiving the theme and flow of a sermon to the time of its delivery, the deeper the impact on my own vision and imaginative relationship to the message. Orality must come from deep within. That process takes time and cannot be rushed.

I have also discovered that orality places a far greater premium upon physical, mental and emotional vitality than does a literary-based sermon. More is required at the moment of delivery. Fatigue will slow the pace, diminish fluency and lessen intensity in an oral preacher. Somehow a manuscript gives, at least to the preacher, a sense of support that may offset the lack of energy to some degree. Orality and good health impress me as being closely linked, particularly for the preacher who gives his sermon more than once on Sunday morning.

Evaluation has become increasingly important to me as I have moved deeper into orality. Even though I have listened to recordings of my preaching for some years, I am finding that this practice is becoming more important than before. Listening early each week to last Sunday's sermon helps me to note problems of pace, of word choice and of meaninglessly repeated phrases ('You know', 'I think', etc.). I also am discovering that occasionally going over the typescript of a sermon brings even greater confrontation with the common foibles of speech. While the ability to remove all the idiosyncrasies of free oral communication will remain beyond my reach, the process of editing does have an enduring power to sensitize me to some of my more noticeable problems.

Above all, orality has brought me to a new awareness that when I stand before a group of listeners with nothing but a Bible in my hand, I am standing as one frail person before needy people with the greatest power in all creation in my possession. Orality increasingly confronts me with the searching question of not only how much I possess God's word but how much God's word possesses me. Lester De Koster reflects this when he writes: 'Vestiges of the Quintillian schema linger on in the "orals" that complete doctoral programs to this day – only what can be orally expressed has been truly mastered.'[4]

This beginning exploration of orality brings me to the vision of preaching that Bishop Quayle described and to which I continue to aspire.

Preaching is the art of making a sermon and delivering it. Why no, that is not preaching. Preaching is the art of making a preacher and delivering that. Preaching is the outrush of soul in speech. Therefore, the elemental business in preaching is not with the preaching but the preacher. It is no trouble to preach, but a vast trouble to construct a preacher. What then, in the light of this, is the task of the preacher? Mainly this, the amassing of a great soul so as to have something worthwhile to give – the sermon is the preacher up to date.[5]

Footnotes

Chapter 2
1. Atchity 1986, 1.
2. Ensign 1985, 1.
3. Ong 1977, 267.
4. Ong 1982, 10.
5. Postman 1985.
6. McLuhan 1970, 83.
7. Carpenter and McLuhan 1960, 65-66.
8. Robinson 1980, 161-162.
9. Buttrick 1987, 86-87.
10. Ong 1977, 57.
11. Ong 1977, 58.
12. Ong 1977, 60-61.
13. Ong 1971, 297.
14. Ong 1977, 87.
15. Ong 1977, 87-88.
16. Ong 1982, 34.
17. Ong 1982, 35.
18. Ong 1971, 299.
19. Ong 1982, 39-40.
20. Ong 1982, 49.
21. Ong 1982, 51-55.
22. Ong 1982, 116.
23. Ong 1982, 12.
24. Ong 1982, 14-15.
25. Naisbitt 1982, 35.
26. Fant 1987, 248.
27. Brigance 1953, 200.
28. Brigance 1953, 200.
29. Brigance 1953, 201.
30. Fant 1987, 161-163.
31. Craddock 1985, 190.
32. Craddock 1985, 191-192.
33. Riesman 1960, 110.
34. Havelock 1986, 70.

Chapter 3
1. Clapp 1996, 135.
2. Peterson 1987, 72.
3. Ong 1982, 32.
4. Peterson 1987, 61.
5. Peterson 1987, 62.
6. Peterson 1987, 62.
7. Peterson 1987, 64.
8. Ong 1967, 19.
9. Larsen 1995, 135.
10. Peterson 1987, 69.
11. Oden 1989, 219.
12. Oden 1989, 219-220.
13. Bloesch 1997, 237-238.
14. Oden 1989, 149.
15. Ellul 1985, 63.
16. Ellul 1985, 97.
17. Ellul 1985, 96.
18. Fant 1987, *xii.*
19. Fant 1987, *xii-xiii.*
20. Meyers 1993, 21.
21. Buechner 1977, 22-23.
22. Fant 1987, 159.
23. Loscalzo 1992, 254.
24. Peterson 1987, 63.
25. Ward 1992, 25-27.
26. Ward 1992, 28.
27. Thielicke 1963, 12.
28. Lewis and Lewis 1983, 149.
29. Decker 1992, 236.
30. Eslinger 1996, 2-3.
31. Willimon and Lischer 1995, 353.
32. Berkley 1986, 62.
33. Jowett 1968, 171-172.
34. Storrs 1875, 13-15.
35. Willimon and Lischer 1995, 134.
36. Willimon and Lischer 1995, 352.
37. Fant 1987, 11.
38. Long 1989, 181.
39. Dale 1905, 157.

Chapter 4
1. Baumann 1972, 194.
2. Fant and Pinson 1971, 10:101.
3. Barth 1991, 119.
4. Baxter 1971, 184.
5. Baxter 1971, 195-196.
6. O'Day and Long 1993, 172-173.
7. Banks and Stevens 1997, 787.
8. Craddock 1985, 170.
9. Wilson 1992, 22.
10. Willimon and Lischer, 1995, 185.
11. Duduit 1992, 410.
12. Willimon and Lischer 1995, 189.
13. Willimon and Lischer 1995, 71.
14. Willimon and Lischer 1995, 70.
15. Willimon and Lischer 1995, 20-21.
16. Fant and Pinson 1971, 1:119.
17. Duduit 1992, 410.
18. Fant and Pinson 1971, 1:147.
19. Fant and Pinson 1971, 1:191-192.
20. Willimon and Lischer 1995, 313.
21. Willimon and Lischer 1995, 205.
22. Fant and Pinson 1971, 2:140.
23. Fant and Pinson 1971, 2:195.
24. Duduit 1992, 410.
25. Broadus 1944, 315.
26. Fant and Pinson 1971, 2:285.
27. Willimon and Lishcher 1995, 133.
28. Lewis 1983, 150-151.

136 THE POWER OF SPEAKING GOD'S WORD

29. Willimon and Lischer 1995, 218.
30. Fant and Pinson 1971, 3:51-52.
31. Murray 1987, 190-191.
32. Fant and Pinson 1971, 3:112.
33. Fant and Pinson 1971, 3:113.
34. Fant and Pinson 1971, III:180-181.
35. Bonar 1854, 38-39.
36. Fant and Pinson 1971, 4:369.
37. Fant and Pinson 1971, 4:370.
38. Fant and Pinson 1971, 4:370.
39. Storrs 1875, 34.
40. Cox 1985, 242.
41. Fant and Pinson 1971, 5:7-8.
42. Cox 1985, 244.
43. Fant and Pinson 1971, 5:56-57.
44. Fant and Pinson 1971, 5:245-246.
45. Fant and Pinson 1971, 6:12.
46. Spurgeon 1972, 141.
47. Spurgeon 1972, 142.
48. Spurgeon 1972, 143.
49. Spurgeon 1972, 152.
50. Burrell 1913, 244.
51. Burrell 1913, 245.
52. Burrell 1913, 245-246.
53. Burrell 1913, 246-251.
54. Burrell 1913, 258.
55. Brown 1931, 84.
56. Brown 1931, 86.
57. Fant and Pinson 1971, 183.
58. Fant and Pinson 1971, 8:11.
59. Fant and Pinson 1971, 8:137-138.
60. Fant and Pinson 1971, 8:230-231.
61. Fant and Pinson 1971, 9:24-25.
62. Fant and Pinson 1971, 9:79.
63. Macartney 1976.
64. Fant and Pinson 1971, 9:114-116.
65. Fant and Pinson 1971, 9:184.
66. Fant and Pinson 1971, 11:149-150.
67. Fant and Pinson 1971, 11:229.
68. Fant and Pinson 1971, 11:230.
69. Sargent 1994, 281.
70. Lloyd-Jones 1971, 83-84.
71. Fant and Pinson 1971, 11:338.
72. Fant and Pinson 1971, 11:338.
73. Fant and Pinson 1971, 12:106.
74. Fant and Pinson 1971, 12:111-112.
75. Fant and Pinson 1971, 12:149.
76. Fant and Pinson 1971, 12:362.
77. Ailes 1988, 32.

Chapter 5
1. Dale 1905, 151.
2. Carruthers 1990, Yates 1966.
3. Ong 1971, 105.

4. Havelock 1986.
5. Ong 1971, 110.
6. Ong 1971, 110-111.
7. Ensign 1985, 97.
8. Sangster 1974, 49.
9. Litchfield 1996.
10. Litchfield 1996, 22.
11. Litchfield 1996, 23.
12. Litchfield 1996, 28.
13. Litchfield 1996, 29.
14. White 1973, 150.
15. Oliver and Cortright 1961, 40.
16. Storrs 1875, 23-24.
17. Macartney 1976, 158-160.
18. Borden 1992.
19. Burrell 1913, 215.
20. Sangster 1976, 61.
21. Chapell 1992, 11.
22. Wiersbe 1994, 81.
23. Wiersbe 1994, 82-83.
24. Wiersbe 1994, 222.
25. Sunukjian 1989, unpublished lecture notes.
26. Adams 1976, 45-46.
27. Chapell 1994, 234.
28. Wilson 1995, 227-236, 243-262.
29. Yates 1966.
30. Fant 1987, 159-161.
31. Fant 1987, 161-162.
32. Fant 1987, 163-164.
33. Fant 1987, 164-165.
34. Barth 1991, 119.
35. Craddock 1985, 189-191.
36. Fant 1987, 165-173.
37. Fant 1987, 166.
38. Fant 1987, 166.
39. Fant 1987, 166.
40. Osborne 1991, 362.
41. Robinson 1989, 174.
42. Fant 1987, 166-167.
43. Fant 1987, 170.
44. Fant 1987, 171.
45. Fant 1987, 173.
46. Koller 1962, 85.

Chapter 6
1. Banks and Stevens 1997, 787.
2. Macartney 1976, 153.
3. Loscalzo 1992, 155.
4. Logan 1986, 312.
5. Turnbull 1967, 57-58.

Bibliography

Adams, Jay E. 1976. *Studies in preaching.* Vol. 3, *Sense appeal on the sermons of Charles Haddon Spurgeon.* Nutley, N.J.: Presbyterian and Reformed Publishing.

Ailes, Roger. 1988. *You are the message.* New York: Doubleday/ Curency.

Atchity, Kenneth. 1986. *A writer's time.* New York: W. W. Norton.

Banks, Robert and R. Paul Stevens. 1997. *The complete book of everyday Christianity.* Downers Grove: InterVarsity.

Barth, Karl. 1991. *Homiletics.* Translated by Geoffrey Bromiley and Donald Daniels. Louisville: Westminster/John Knox.

Bartow, Charles L. 1980. *The preaching moment: A guide to sermon delivery.* Nashville: Abingdon.

Baumann, J. Daniel. 1972. *An introduction to contemporary preaching.* Grand Rapids: Baker.

Baxter, Batsell Barrett. 1971. *The heart of the Yale lectures.* Grand Rapids: Baker.

Berkley, James D., ed. 1986. *Preaching to convince.* Waco: Leadership/Word.

Bloesch, Donald. 1997. *Jesus Christ: Savior and Lord.* Downers Grove, IL: InterVarsity.

Bonar, Andrew A. 1854. *The life and remains, letters, lectures, and poems of the Rev. Robert Murray McCheyne.* New York: Robert Carter and Brothers.

Borden, Paul. Unpublished lecture notes. Denver Seminary, Denver. 1992.

Brigance, William Norwood. 1953. *Speech composition.* 2nd ed. New York: Appleton-Century-Crofts.

Broadus, John A. 1944. *On the preparation and delivery of sermons.* Revised by Jesse Burton Weatherspoon. New York: Harper.

Brown, Charles R. 1931. *My own yesterdays.* New York: Century.

Buechner, Frederick. 1977. *Telling the truth.* New York: Harper and Row.

Burrell, David James. 1913. *The sermon: its construction and delivery.* New York: Fleming H. Revell.

Buttrick, David. 1987. *Homiletic.* Philadelphia: Fortress.

Carpenter, Edmund and, Marshall McLuhan, eds. 1960. *Exploration in communication.* Boston: Beacon.

Carruthers, Mary. 1990. *The book of memory: a study of memory in Medieval culture.* Cambridge and New York: Cambridge University Press.

Chapell, Bryan. 1994. *Christ-centered preaching* Grand Rapids: Baker.

_____. 1992. *Using illustrations to preach with power.* Grand Rapids: Zondervan.

Clapp, Rodney. 1996. *A peculiar people: the church as culture in a post-Christian society.* Downers Grove: InterVarsity.

Cox, James W. 1985. *Preaching.* San Francisco: Harper and Row.

Craddock, Fred B. 1978. *Overhearing the gospel.* Nashville: Abingdon.

_____. 1985. *Preaching.* Nashville: Abingdon.

Dale, R.W. 1905. *Nine lectures on preaching.* London: Hodder and Stoughton.

Davis, Henry Grady. 1958. *Design for preaching.* Philadelphia: Fortress.

Decker, Bert. 1992. *You've got to be believed to be heard.* New York: St. Martin's Press.

Duduit, Michael, ed. 1992. *Handbook of contemporary preaching.* Nashville: Broadman.

Ellul, Jacques. 1985. *The humilation of the word.* Grand Rapids: Eerdmans.

Ensign, Robert A. 1985. *Talking it to life.*Ph.D.diss.,Emory University.

Eslinger, Richard L. 1996. *Pitfalls in preaching.* Grand Rapids: Eerdmans.

Fant, Clyde E., Jr. 1987. *Preaching for today.* New York: Harper and Row.

Fant, Clyde E. and William M. Pinson, Jr., eds. 1971. *20 centuries of great preaching.* Waco: Word.

Farrer, Austin. 1949. *A rebirth of images.* Glasgow: University Press; reprint, Westminster: Dacre Press, n.d.

Havelock, Eric A. 1986. *The muse learns to write.* New Haven: Yale University Press.

Jowett, J. H. 1968. *The preacher: his life and work.* n.p. George H. Doran Company, 1912; reprint, Grand Rapids: Baker.

Koller, Charles W. 1962. *Expository preaching without notes.* Grand Rapids: Baker.

Larsen, David L. 1989. *The anatomy of preaching.* Grand Rapids: Baker.

_____. 1995. *Telling the old, old story.* Wheaton: Crossway.

Lewis, Ralph L. with Gregg Lewis. 1983: *Inductive preaching.* Wheaton: Crossway.

Litchfield, Hugh. 1996. *Visualizing the sermon: a guide to preaching without notes.* Sioux Falls: Hugh Litchfield.

Lloyd-Jones, D. Martyn. 1971. *Preaching and preachers.* Grand Rapids: Zondervan.

Logan, Samuel T., ed. 1986. *The preacher and preaching.* Phillipsburg, N.J.: Presbyterian and Reformed Publishing.

Long, Thomas G. 1988. *The senses of preaching.* Atlanta: John Knox Press.

Loscalzo, Craig A. 1992. *Preaching sermons that connect.* Downers Grove, IL: InterVarsity.

Macartney, Clarence E. 1976. *Preaching without notes.* n.p. Stone and Pierce, 1946; reprint, Grand Rapids: Baker.

Mawhinney, Bruce. 1991. *Preaching with freshness.* Eugene, OR.: Harvest House.

McLuhan, Marshall. 1970. *From cliché to archetype.* New York: The Viking Press.

Meyers, Robin R. 1993. *With ears to hear.* Cleveland: The Pilgrim Press.

Murray, Iain H. 1987. *Jonathan Edwards.* Carlisle, Pa.: The Banner of Truth Trust.

Naisbitt, John. 1982. *Megatrends.* New York: Warner.

O'Day, Gail R. and Thomas G. Long, eds. 1993. *Listening to the Word: studies in honor of Fred B. Craddock.* Nashville: Abingdon.

Oden, Thomas C. 1989. *The word of life.* San Francisco: Harper Collins.

Oliver, Robert T. and Rupert L. Cortright. 1961. *Effective speech.* 2nd ed. New York: Holt, Rinehart and Winston.

Ong, Walter J. 1967. *The presence of the word.* New Haven: Yale University Press.

_____. 1971. *Rhetoric, romance, and technology.* Ithaca and London: Cornell University Press.

_____. 1977. *Interfaces of the word.* Ithaca and London: Cornell University Press.

_____. 1982. *Orality and literacy: The technologizing of the word.* London and New York: Methuen.

Osborne, Grant. 1991. *The hermeneutical spiral.* Downers Grove, IL : InterVarsity.

Peterson, Eugene. 1987. *Working the angles.* Grand Rapids: Eerdmans.

Pitt-Watson, Ian. 1986. *A primer for preachers.* Grand Rapids: Baker.

Postman, Neil. 1985. *Amusing ourselves to death.* New York: Penguin.

Riesman, David. 1960. 'The Oral and Written Tradition' *Explorations in communication.* ed: Edmund Carpenter and Marshall McLuhan. Boston: Beacon.

Robinson, Haddon W., 1980. *Biblical preaching.* Grand Rapids: Baker.

Robinson, Haddon W., ed. 1989. *Biblical sermons.* Grand Rapids: Baker.

Sangster, W. E. 1972. *The craft of sermon construction.* n.p. W.L. Jenkins, 1951; reprint, Grand Rapids: Baker.

_____. 1974. *The approach to preaching.* n.p. W. L. Jenkins, 1952; reprint, Grand Rapids: Baker.

_____. 1976. *Power in preaching.* n.p. Epworth Press, 1958; Reprint, Grand Rapids: Baker.

Sargent, Tony. 1994. *The sacred anointing:* Wheaton. Crossway.

Spurgeon, Charles Haddon. 1972. *Lectures to my students.* reprint, Grand Rapids: Zondervan.

Stevenson, Dwight E. and Charles F. Diehl. 1958. *Reaching people from the pulpit: A guide to effective sermon delivery.* New York: Harper.

Storrs, Richard S. 1875. *Conditions of success in preaching without notes.* New York: Dodd, Mead & Co.

Sunukjian, Donald. Unpublished lecture notes. Deerfield: Trinity Evangelical Divinity School. 1989.

Sweazy, George E. 1976. *Preaching the good news.* Englewood Cliffs, NJ: Prentice-Hall.

Thielicke, Helmut. 1963. A personal letter printed in *Christianity Today.* October 25, 1963:12.

Turnbull, Ralph G., ed. 1967. *Baker's dictionary of practical theology.* Grand Rapids: Baker.

Ward, Richard F. 1992. *Speaking from the heart.* Nashville: Abingdon.

White, R. E. O. 1973. *A guide to preaching.* Grand Rapids: Eerdmans.

Whitesell, Faris D. 1963. *Power in expository preaching.* Old Tappan, NJ: Fleming H. Revell.

Wiersbe, Warren W. 1994. *Preaching and teaching with imagination.* Wheaton: Victor.

Willimon, William H. and Richard Lischer, eds. 1995. *Concise encyclopedia of preaching.* Louisville: Westminster/John Knox Press.

Wilson, Paul Scott. 1992. *A concise history of preaching.* Nashville: Abingdon.

_____. 1995. *The practice of preaching.* Nashville: Abingdon.

Yates, Frances A. 1966. *The art of memory.* Chicago: The University of Chicago Press.

Scripture Index

Persons Index

Subject Index